GW01398883

A Journey T
Healthcare

A Story of Health, Family and Human Values

By
Gopi Paladugu

Copyright © 2024

All Rights Reserved

Disclaimer

The stories and characters in this book are purely fictional. Any resemblance to real persons, living or dead, or actual events is entirely coincidental.

Dedication

To my parents, my wife, and my daughter.

To all the healthcare workers and amazing patients.

Acknowledgments

Gwen Witzel for reviewing the book.

Sharath Chandra Paladugu for giving suggestions.

Sai Shristi Paladugu, thank you for encouraging and supporting me.

About the Author

Gopi Paladugu has over a decade of experience working as a physician. Throughout his medical practice, he has encountered numerous patients with a variety of questions and has observed the common challenges faced by patients and their families in navigating the healthcare system. Over the years, he has witnessed both the strengths and weaknesses of healthcare. He has consistently emphasized the importance of primary care, mental health, medication compliance, and lifestyle changes.

In his new book, Dr. Paladugu aims to share his insights in a manner that is simple and easy to understand to the public. He delves into the significance of family values and their impact on healthcare, especially in the context of caring for elderly parents. Drawing from his own experiences, he underscores the importance of human values in healthcare and the community.

The book also addresses crucial topics such as advanced care planning, hospice, and palliative care, reflecting his experience as a Hospice physician. He also highlights the challenges and importance of rural health based on his understanding of the difficulties faced by patients in rural America.

As a clinical professor involved in teaching medical students and residents, Dr. Paladugu brings a wealth of knowledge to his writing. He also holds advanced degrees in Clinical Nutrition, Strategic Management, and Business Administration. Additionally, he has completed several certification courses in healthcare quality, patient experience, hospice care, and artificial intelligence in medicine. His expertise in clinical nutrition allows him to address important topics like obesity and lifestyle changes, while his business education provides insight into the financial aspects of healthcare.

In his role as a Physician Advisor in Utilization Management, Dr. Paladugu has gained a deep understanding of the health insurance landscape. He is passionate about improving healthcare quality, safety, and patient experience, having worked on numerous projects related to these areas. This experience has reinforced his belief in the importance of value-based care.

Dr. Paladugu's book is designed to address the common questions and challenges patients face during their healthcare journey while also highlighting the importance of human values and family support. Using relatable stories and emotional narratives, he conveys complex topics in a way that is easy for laypeople to understand.

Join Gopi Paladugu on this enlightening journey and discover a new way to appreciate the world of healthcare through his fascinating storytelling.

Contents

Chapter 1

It was a typical November morning on John's farmstead in rural Illinois. The winter sunbathed the Midwest in a golden glow, but the trees were stripped of their leaves. Their once vibrant red and orange leaves are now gone. Only the occasional crow or creak of wind through the wooden fences disturbed the stillness. The world seemed so calm; it felt as if nothing bad could ever touch it, and no one could ever know grief.

John mirrored this tranquility, humming along to Rod Stewart's 'I Don't Want to Talk About It' playing on the radio. The familiar melody and lyrics seemed to capture his own melancholy mood as he watched the trees sway gently in the breeze. All was peaceful yet bare as if mirroring his current frame of mind.

He was in his quaint kitchen, carefully cutting pumpkin slices from the bushel on the counter. As he worked, his thoughts drifted to his granddaughter, Sam. Last time, she devoured two slices of his pumpkin pie, exclaiming it was the best she'd ever had. John smiled, remembering her joy and thinking of the secret ingredient that made his pie so special.

John deftly rolled out the pie dough, shaping it into a thin, even circle. Over the decades, he had perfected his pie crust to be light and flaky. But it was what he added to the filling that really made it extraordinary. While others used mainly pumpkin, cinnamon, and nutmeg, John also stirred in a splash of Bourbon. Just enough to enhance the flavors without overpowering them.

John sprinkled the bourbon-laced pumpkin mixture with a pinch of cinnamon before pouring the mixture into the pie shell. The air was filled with the warm aroma of cinnamon and nutmeg. When it was baked, the bourbon would have infused through each bite of the pie. John knew Sam would be delighted, and the secret ingredient would make it a pie she'd savor and remember.

As he worked, his wife, Martha, came strolling in.

"Honey, are you done yet?"

"No, not yet," John answered cheerfully. "But soon, you'll taste the best pies in the whole world."

Martha laughed at his joke. She thought he was hilarious, and with the kind smile that emitted from her lips just then, it was obvious that she loved him like no other. John was a hearty man—a man incapable of being disliked. He radiated a unique positive energy wherever he went, even in the kitchen right now. Still smiling to herself, Martha went to work at her infamous pudding and took in the smell wafting in the air.

"You certainly seem ready for Thanksgiving," she remarked.

"Oh, I am more than ready," John chuckled.

The couple had three children: Henry, Cara, and Michael. The elder, Henry, lived an hour's drive away, so coming to their house for such events was effortless for him. His wife, Lisa, was a wonderful cook and always helped Martha prepare the big feast.

Then came John and Martha's second child, their first daughter, Cara. She had made New York City her home. She worked hard as an executive in the banking sector. John fondly remembered Cara's busy life in New York. She rarely finds time to visit her old hometown these days. He remembered when she was young and would help John and Martha decorate the house and help with food preparations for Thanksgiving.

While Cara stayed in touch as much as her hectic schedule allowed, calling her parents once in a while to check in, Michael's move to Los Angeles had been one of struggle and uncertainty. Eager to pursue his dreams in film and music, Michael uprooted there with his then-girlfriend Ashley to study at the university. But settling in proved difficult as work in their desired fields was scarce. For years, they scraped by, taking whatever jobs they could find while continuing to chase opportunities in .the entertainment industry.

"Martha," John spoke, referring to the memories of their children and how joyful Thanksgivings were when they were around. The family hadn't gathered together for Thanksgiving in years. They eagerly wait to spend time with their family. But work and other life commitments sent them to distant places. Every year, they invite them to come to their house for Thanksgiving. Henry and his family always visit them, while Cara and Michael's family are a miss for Thanksgiving celebrations.

John was giving the final touches to his pumpkin pie. His chest suddenly hurt, but he dismissed it in just a second. They were nothing new to him—his chest burned. He had been experiencing them a lot more now that he was old, and since none of them had resulted in anything alarming, he went on as if nothing happened.

"I will make sure our entire family is together for next year's Thanksgiving," he said, opening his mouth to tell her another memory that he had just recalled when he paused.

And winced—*again*.

This time, the pain seemed severe. John groaned in pain and clutched his chest. John gasped for breath, struggling to catch his breath. His entire world was spinning.

His loyal golden retriever, Scruffy, who had been by John's side since it was a puppy, was the only one who perked up in concern; Martha was still too busy with her custard. Scruffy nudged at John's leg with his nose and gave him a worried look with his dark brown eyes. John wasn't acting like his usual playful self, and Scruffy sensed there was a problem.

Before John could react to the worsening pain, everything started to fade into black. Sheer black. The kind of black that John would gladly stay away from.

But soon, that black pulled him to itself, and he lost consciousness rapidly. He fell on the floor, but thankfully, he did not sustain a head injury. He did not show any other signs of external injuries.

At this, Scruffy started to bark loudly without stopping, interrupting Martha's preparations for the Thanksgiving meal. Martha was worried when Scruffy started barking so loudly. She turned around and saw John lying still on the floor. She hurriedly went to pick him up and started calling his name, but he did not answer. Martha realized something was seriously wrong with John. She wasted no time picking up the phone and steadied her hands enough to call 911 for emergency help.

"Please send an ambulance right away!" Martha said to the operator, straining to keep her voice calm. "My husband has fallen unconscious and isn't waking up."

Martha usually does not ask for help. She got scared and anxious about John's medical emergency. She also picked up her phone and urgently called her firstborn, Henry. She explained the entire ordeal to him, her voice laced with fear and pain.

Henry and his family were getting ready to come to his parents' home. Hearing about his father being in such a state hit him intensely. John—the man who always appeared so full of life and vigor and had taught Henry the importance of diligent work and maintaining humor—was now in a critical condition.

Henry quickly informed his wife, Lisa, and daughter, Sam, of the situation before rushing outside to get in his car. He quickly drove towards his childhood home. Thoughts of potential negative outcomes occupied his mind during the entire drive.

The long wait for the medical team to arrive dragged on endlessly, and every minute that passed only twisted Martha's nerves into tighter knots. Finally, after 30 minutes of frantic waiting, she could hear a familiar wail of siren sounding in the distance. Tears were running down her wrinkled cheeks, and both fear and fragile hope swelled in Martha's mind. The crunching sounds of tires from the gravel on their circular drive announced the arrival of the ambulance.

With his heart faltering and lying unconscious on the floor, John clings to hope like a lifeline. But in the vast expanse of rural America, where the roads stretch like endless ribbons, and help feels miles away, every second without aid feels like an eternity.

The Emergency Medical Services (EMS) volunteers arrived, everyday heroes driven by compassion and a sense of duty. Racing against time, they barrel down winding roads, their sirens piercing the silence of the countryside.

With each bump in the road, they're not just navigating terrain; they're fighting for John's life.

Finally, they arrive, their presence a ray of hope breaking through the storm clouds of uncertainty. But their battle has only just begun. In these forgotten corners of the country, where doctors are a rarity, every decision they make carries the weight of a thousand lives.

Yet, even as they work their magic, the shadows of struggle loom large. In rural America, where healthcare is a luxury rather than a guarantee, the shortage of physicians leaves communities vulnerable and afraid. Yet, hope flickered in the darkness.

Programs like the rural track initiatives call out to the hearts of aspiring healers, urging them to step into the breach and shine their light in the darkest corners of the country. Though the road ahead is fraught with obstacles, from financial burdens to family obligations, they press on, fueled by a sense of duty and compassion that knows no bounds.

So, as we journey through the maze of healthcare in rural America, let us not forget the unsung heroes who labor in the shadows. Let us honor the EMS volunteers who brave the unknown and the physicians, nurses, and other health care professionals who stand as rays of hope in the darkest of nights. For in their hands lies the power to heal, to comfort, and to save lives. And in their hearts beats the rhythm of humanity, lighting the way for us all.

"Where's our patient?" Two paramedics swiftly entered the room with practiced coordination. They obtained information about John's symptoms and health status from Martha. Paramedics checked John's vital signs like blood pressure, pulse and respiratory rate. One of the paramedics placed an intravenous line and started intravenous fluids.

As they further examined John's condition, Martha observed her husband's lively face losing color. His pulse, which had a regular beat just before, began irregularly decreasing at a concerning rate. The kitchen was filled with the sounds of machinery, and the responders were working hastily to get a grip on the emergency.

"His heart has stopped!" one of the paramedics stated with urgency. He wasted no time and started chest compressions. Other paramedics applied defibrillator pads and switched on the defibrillator. The heart rhythm on the defibrillator monitor initially did not suggest delivering a shock to John. The paramedic also took a breathing device from her kit and placed it on John's face. They also gave an injection of epinephrine, an important medicine used during cardiac arrest.

After two minutes of chest compressions, they paused and checked for pulse. "There is still no pulse," said the paramedic. Another paramedic again looked at the heart rhythm on the defibrillator monitor and said we should deliver a shock to the patient. She said, "Stay clear," loudly, and pressed the button on the machine to deliver the shock.

They started chest compressions and applied the breathing device again without wasting any time. After another two minutes of chest compressions, they checked the pulse again. The paramedic exclaimed, "I can feel the pulse!" They looked at the monitor, and John had a regular heart rhythm again.

John regained consciousness and began to move. Paramedics asked questions, and he answered them correctly. John reached out his hand towards Martha and said, "I will be alright."

Martha breathed a sigh of relief. Her racing heart slowed down. She replied, "You will be alright, my love." You can't leave me yet. We have many more years to live together."

Paramedics asked John more questions about his symptoms. They did an electrocardiogram (EKG), looked at it, and said, "John has EKG changes suggestive of a heart attack." They gave him aspirin and a tablet to keep under his tongue. We must take John to the hospital for further workup.

John agreed. Martha kissed John on the forehead and said, "You will be alright. They will take good care of you. I will meet you at the hospital." They placed John on a stretcher and moved him into the ambulance.

Henry drove up to the old family home just before the paramedics took John to the hospital. "Dad, how are you doing?" John answered, "Oh! I am fine. Pumpkin pie is almost done, and Sam will like it," Henry said with a smile.

A sense of relief came over Henry at the sight of John. When Martha saw Henry, tears welled in her eyes, and she gripped him tightly in a long hug. Henry's presence provided Martha with comfort and reassurance.

"I'll meet you at the hospital," Martha told John as she watched the paramedics drive the ambulance past them.

Within the empty house, an unnatural stillness filled the air. It starkly contrasted with the joyful holiday atmosphere that John had hoped to create for this year's Thanksgiving. Always lively, Scruffy was also unusually quiet. Henry placed Scruffy in his kennel. Henry and Martha got into their car and drove to the hospital.

While driving, Henry thought about his prior conversations with John regarding visiting a primary care doctor for his health checkups. John used to visit his primary care doctor regularly. He developed a good relationship and trust with his doctor. The doctor became old and approached his retirement. He wanted to sell his practice to another doctor, but no one was willing to buy it and settle in this rural area. The doctor finally sold it to a nearby health system.

Since the doctor left, John has never developed a consistent relationship with his doctor. Other doctors came for a short time and left before John could trust them. He stopped going to his doctor's visits and taking his medicines.

After an hour's drive, Martha and Henry reached the hospital.

Martha began to feel exhaustion overtaking her. She and Henry took seats in the emergency room, waiting at the hospital. She replayed the sequence of frightening events in her mind: John suddenly collapsing, her frantic phone call for help, and the torturous wait for the ambulance to arrive, which left her worried and sick.

Now, sitting there, surrounded by sterile hospital walls and equipment, she started to long for the warmth and familiarity of her home. Henry did his best to console his mother, hoping to receive an update soon from the doctors on John's condition and whether the medical care here would improve his chances of recovery or not.

Martha grasped Henry's hand firmly, seeking his reassurance.

"Do you think your father will be okay?" She asked in a quiet, shaky, worried voice.

Henry, always the stable foundation of support for his loved ones, gave his mother's hand a comforting squeeze in response. "We don't know for sure yet, Mom," he acknowledged truthfully. "But the medical team here is highly skilled. Dad is receiving the best possible care available in this area right now."

Mother and son reminisced about happier times of John's playful spirit. His ability to always find humor in any situation to lift their spirits. Recalling happier times from when they were growing up helped lift their emotions, even if just for a brief moment.

Just then, Henry's phone lit up with a call from Mary. She is Henry's neighbor. She worked as a primary care physician in a rural clinic. Henry answered the phone. "Hi Mary, how are you? Lisa told me your dad is having some medical problems. How is he doing now? How're you guys holding up?

He is fine. Henry explained that day's events to Mary. He is brought to the local hospital for further workup. We are waiting for an update from the doctor. With steady hands and unwavering determination, paramedics worked tirelessly to save John and gave him a fighting chance against the odds.

Mary replied that EMS personnel are the backbone of the community's health and safety. She talked about the increasing demand for emergency medical personnel in rural areas and empathized deeply with the hardships faced by EMS volunteers. She believed in the power of inspiring younger generations to volunteer for EMS services. The limited funding, vast coverage areas, and demanding nature of their roles only strengthened their resolve.

Providing these selfless individuals with comprehensive training, robust financial support, and meaningful incentives was crucial to attracting and retaining them, ensuring the continued provision of life-saving care in their rural communities.

Mary recognized that in life-threatening situations like heart attacks, strokes, accidents, and opioid overdoses, every precious minute mattered. With a sense of urgency, Mary passionately emphasized the pressing need for policy changes to ensure fair and adequate reimbursement for the invaluable services provided by EMS providers.

Is the local hospital still open? Mary questioned. "Yes, we are fortunate to have it still open," replied Henry.

Martha continued, "I read in the newspaper that they are having a hard time finding staff to work—their costs are increasing, and reimbursements are decreasing. These facilities serve as beacons of comprehensive care and lifelines for their rural areas, providing essential medical services and specialized treatments that are otherwise difficult to access, but many rural hospitals across the country are closing due to financial challenges."

Mary also talked about the profound impact of healthcare shortages in rural areas. She expressed frustration over the shortage of local primary care clinics in rural areas compared to urban areas, where they need them the most. Rural communities have more uninsured and sick people. Life expectancy is lower in rural areas than in urban areas.

It is challenging to recruit and retain a physician in a rural community. It can be hard to practice medicine since you might be the only physician with limited laboratory, radiology, and specialist support. There might be limited schooling and extracurricular activities for their children. Sometimes, spouses can have a hard time finding jobs matching their skills in the rural community. Also, many physicians practicing in rural communities are old, and as they retire, the health care shortage in these communities will get even worse, said Mary.

As a rural physician, she knew just how much the relationships physicians built with their patients mattered. Doctors who are from rural areas are more likely to make rural communities their home and practice medicine in these communities. These personal connections were the lifeblood of rural healthcare, influencing the decision of healthcare professionals to stay and serve despite the challenges.

Mary kept a keen eye on the government's efforts to address the issue, eagerly following the progress of initiatives, such as expanding medical schools and residency programs and allocating funds for rural healthcare. Nurse practitioners, physician assistants under the guidance of physicians, and internationally trained physicians who work through exchange waiver programs are also playing a critical role in bridging some of these care gaps.

These trained professionals are stepping in to provide medical services ranging from routine health checkups to providing specialized care in these communities that may lack full-time physicians.

Mary also expressed optimism regarding the impact of technology on improving rural health access, such as telemedicine services through remote consultations and the use of electronic health records for better exchange of health information. As access to the internet and digital literacy improves, technology can have a significant impact on improving rural health access.

Let me end the call on a positive note. Call me anytime if you need help, said Mary. Henry thanked Mary for the call and for providing useful information.

Listening to Mary, Henry clearly understood how much a quality healthcare system in small communities can impact people's lives and outcomes. What may have seemed like an abstract issue before now had a personal meaning as he saw firsthand how it affected his dad. Henry was grateful for the medical team helping his father, but he also recognized how their community's limitations in basic services could prove detrimental in other cases.

Henry and Martha sat in the emergency room waiting area, keeping an anxious watch over what seemed like an endless stretch of time. The sole noises around them were the rhythmic ticking of the wall clock and the soft voices of staff working nearby. The harsh fluorescent lights of the waiting room washed everything in a pale-yellow glow that made Henry feel unwell. He fidgeted restlessly on the scratchy plastic chair, his sneakers squeaking against the hard floor as he shifted around nervously. A glance at his mother showed deep lines of worry etched into her face, deeper than he had ever seen before. Her usually bright blue eyes looked dull and drained as she stared unmoving at her worn copy of Reader's Digest sitting unused in her lap.

The air felt heavy and still, carrying the sharp scent of disinfectant that clashed bitterly with the stale coffee brewing somewhere down the hall. Through the thin walls came muffled coughs and beeping machines, a constant backdrop reminding them of the activity happening out of sight behind closed doors. Every so often, the automatic doors would slide open with a hiss, releasing a tired doctor or stressed nurse with no answers showing on their faces.

During this growing chaos, Martha longed for the familiar creak of their porch swings back home, needing anything to drown out the unsettling sounds around them in the hospital waiting room. After what felt like endless waiting, the doctor at last came through the doors from the emergency room area. His expression revealed nothing about the news he brought.

A flicker of hope pierced the gloom of doubt. John had survived. His condition is now stable. Relief momentarily shone on Martha's face as Henry's eyes showed a subtle spark of resolve. He knew that this marked only the beginning. The doctor continued explaining the tests they performed.

John has elevated troponin. Troponin is a protein that can be elevated in conditions like heart attack. Troponin elevation itself does not mean John has a heart attack. His electrocardiogram also showed changes suggestive of a heart attack. We started him on a blood thinner. My suggestion is that we should send him to the tertiary hospital in the city, where he can get further cardiac workup.

John consented to go to a specialized hospital for more advanced treatment. The emergency physician called the other hospital and reported John's medical condition. John is airlifted to the tertiary hospital for specialized cardiac care.

Chapter 2

Michael, the youngest child of Martha and John, lived with his wife Ashley in California. Since high school, Michael was very talented at playing the guitar. His fingers moved effortlessly across the strings, producing melodies that were both intricate and soulful. He had an innate ability to improvise, often creating beautiful compositions on the spot. His understanding of music theory was advanced for his age, allowing him to play a wide range of genres, from classical to rock.

Michael's performances were not just about technical proficiency—he played with a passion that could move his audience, conveying deep emotions through his instrument. He could make the guitar sing, weep, or express joy, making each performance a unique and memorable experience.

On the other hand, Ashley, who was his girlfriend at the time, was an amazing dancer and actor. Ashley moved with natural grace and fluidity, whether she was performing a delicate ballet piece or a high-energy hip-hop routine. Her dance skills were complemented by her exceptional acting talent.

Ashley was a versatile actress who could bring any character to life. She had an expressive face and a powerful presence on stage, which allowed her to communicate complex emotions without saying a word. Her performances captivated the audience, holding their attention from start to finish. She was also highly versatile, seamlessly transitioning between different dance styles and acting genres. Her dedication to her craft was evident in every performance, making her a standout talent in both dance and theater.

A fun fact was that Ashley was in the same class as Cara, John's, and Martha's daughter, while Michael was a year younger than them in school.

It was during the high school production of Romeo and Juliet that Ashley and Michael participated as the main characters. Michael played Romeo, and Ashley played Juliet. The atmosphere during rehearsals was electric, with the stage adorned in period-appropriate decor, complete with elaborate backdrops of Verona. Every day after school, they would meet in the dimly lit auditorium, its old wooden seats creaking under the weight of time and history. The smell of paint and sawdust from the set pieces mingled with the faint scent of Ashley's floral perfume.

There was an undeniable chemistry between Michael and Ashley. Their most romantic scene, the balcony scene, was where they felt the connection most strongly. Michael would gaze up at Ashley, standing on a makeshift balcony, her eyes sparkling under the stage lights. He would pour his heart out in poetic verses, his voice steady and filled with emotion. Ashley, in turn, would look down at him with a mix of longing and tenderness, her voice soft yet powerful as she spoke Juliet's lines.

With each rehearsal, their interactions grew more natural and intimate. They began to see each other not just as their characters but as real people with genuine feelings. The stage became a place where they could explore their emotions freely. The audience may have seen Romeo and Juliet, but what was blossoming was the real love story between Michael and Ashley.

Ashley dreamed of going to Los Angeles to pursue her passion for dance and music. Michael also decided to go to Los Angeles to study music since Ashley was going there. Ashley waited a year after completing her schooling for Michael to finish high school so that they could go to Los Angeles together. After completing college, they decided to stay in Los Angeles to pursue careers in movies. They got married and settled there.

Initially, they struggled to establish their careers. Moving from a rural area to a major city, they were unprepared for the challenges and competition. They did their best but couldn't get many offers in movies.

They picked up any small assignments that came their way. They worked in restaurants and grocery stores and performed music gigs at local bars to earn money. Even during their tough times, they never gave up. Especially during one college semester, they did not have enough money for both Ashley and Michael to continue their education. Michael had to take a break from college for that semester.

Facing tough situations can reveal your character and human values. They never lost sight of their target. They saved as much money as they could. With hard work and determination, they finally established their own music and dance school, permanently settling in Los Angeles. Later, they had two daughters, Emily and Sofia.

Michael and his family did not visit their rural hometown after moving to Los Angeles. John and Martha never saw their two granddaughters except in photos and videos.

John and Martha often thought about meeting Michael and his family and spending time with their grandchildren.

However, sadly, they never got the chance. The absence of their family felt much bigger now that sudden suffering had befallen their home, and John was taken to the hospital.

***

John was admitted to the tertiary hospital in the city. The hospitalist took a detailed history from John and entered the admission orders. Hospitalists manage patients from admission to discharge, consulting with specialists as needed. The hospitalist ran more tests, including an echocardiogram. The echocardiogram revealed that John's heart wasn't pumping as efficiently as it should. His heart also showed wall motion abnormalities where certain areas of his heart wall moved less compared to other areas of his heart wall.

John was continued on the blood thinner and connected to a telemetry device to monitor his heart rate and rhythm. "John, your blood sugar and blood pressure readings are running high. I will start you on medicines to lower them. I will also consult a cardiologist to check on you since you had a heart attack," explained the hospitalist.

John was evaluated by the cardiologists at the hospital. The cardiologist suggested doing cardiac catheterization. "Cardiac catheterization is a procedure where the cardiologist injects dye to take pictures. The dye flows through the blood vessels that supply the heart," the cardiologist explained.

John agreed to get a cardiac catheterization. He was found to have three blocked blood vessels that supply blood to the heart. The cardiologist informed him, "Based on the cardiac catheterization report, you will require coronary artery bypass grafting surgery. It will involve opening the chest and bypassing the blood flow around the blocked blood vessels using blood vessels from another part of the body."

John wanted to think about it and ultimately, he talked to Martha and Henry. Martha and Henry keenly listened to him. Concern grew on their faces as they learned more about John's condition. They never imagined that John would face all these medical challenges. This was the first time someone from their family had been taken to the hospital for serious heart disease, and they had little to no knowledge about how to tackle the situation. They remained supportive nonetheless.

After discussing this with his family, John agreed to get coronary artery bypass graft surgery. The hospitalist consulted a cardiothoracic surgeon to evaluate the patient.

The surgeon evaluated John's medical records, including the cardiac catheterization report, and informed them that John would need cardiac bypass surgery. The surgeon explained in detail the risks and benefits associated with the surgery. John and his family asked more questions about the surgery, and the surgeon answered them in detail.

After listening to the surgeon, John agreed to the bypass surgery after understanding the risks and benefits. The surgeon ordered a few more tests, like a CT chest scan, an ultrasound of neck vessels, and a test to assess lung function. The surgeon also wanted John's blood pressure and blood sugar to be better controlled prior to taking him to surgery.

After the surgeon left, Henry called his wife Lisa and Sam since they hadn't gotten an update about what was going on with John. Sam was close to her "Big Grandpa." She used to come and spend several days with John and Martha at their house. Henry explained John's diagnosis and the recommended treatment plan. Listening to her dad, Sam was stressed because her dearest grandpa was not in the best shape; he had dangerously high blood pressure and blood sugar levels and would need big surgery. Lisa consoled her daughter and encouraged her to stay positive. Sam prayed for a speedy recovery of her "Big Grandpa."

The doctors were trying their best to adjust medications to control John's blood pressure and blood sugar. The lab and other workup results ordered by the surgeon came back. John was medically optimized and cleared to get cardiac bypass surgery.

John and Martha's friends made phone calls to get updates about John's health status. They also sent flowers and cards, wishing him the best of luck for the cardiac bypass surgery and a speedy recovery. Their friends have been in their lives for several years. They were part of their important life events, and they shared several memories together. Be it happiness or hardships. Their friends were with them to provide support. John and Martha love playing card games with their friends. During weekends, their card games usually extend into late nights.

As their children moved to distant places, their friendships got even stronger. They relied on each other for emotional support and companionship. These friendships were a source of strength as John and Martha navigated this journey of their lives together.

Finally, it was time for the surgery. As Martha and Henry sat in the waiting area, they continued praying for John to get better. There was growing nervousness, tension, and concern. At the same time, they couldn't help but think about what could have been done to avoid this situation.

Fortunately, the surgery went well, without any major complications. The cardiothoracic surgeon did a great job. John was transferred to the intensive care unit for close monitoring. Several intravenous lines and catheters were connected to John—John was recovering well after the bypass surgery.

The medical team was dedicated to John's recovery, focusing on some of the crucial aspects of his health. Physical therapy and Occupational therapy performed their initial assessments. They encouraged John to get up and move around safely as much as possible to prevent blood clots and keep his muscles strong.

The medical team also emphasized preventing mental confusion while in the hospital. Simple measures like keeping the window blinds open during the day, preventing constipation and urinary retention, controlling pain better, avoiding dehydration and maintaining normal electrolytes can help preserve John's mental clarity.

John's care also reflected the balance of medications and mentation. The medical staff tried to limit the use of strong pain medications to avoid confusion, respiratory depression and drowsiness. John was not taking any medications prior to this hospitalization. John is now started on several new medications. The medical team also watched closely for drug interactions and side effects from these medications.

When the nurse asked John what mattered most to him, he chuckled and expressed his desire to make a speedy recovery and leave the hospital as soon as possible.

John's condition was improving, his pain was manageable, and his blood pressure and blood sugar readings were stable. Martha and Henry were happy with the overall progress.

But then, seven days into hospitalization, his recovery took a back step. Suddenly, John started developing fevers and chills. His pulse rate increased, he was breathing fast, and his blood pressure was running on the lower side. The nurse informed Martha and Henry, "I will ask the hospitalist to come and examine John. He does not look good to me. I will also activate the rapid response team."

The hospitalist and rapid response team examined John and ordered tests like a chest X-ray, lactic acid, and blood cultures. The hospitalist informed John, "You are having sepsis. Sepsis is your body's reaction to an infection. Sepsis is a dangerous medical condition and one of the leading causes of death in hospitals.

There is redness around the large intravenous line called the central venous catheter that we are using to give medicines. It looks infected. I will order intravenous fluids and antibiotics. We will wait for the blood work results to come back. If your low blood pressure doesn't improve with intravenous fluids and antibiotics, then I might order intravenous medicines called vasopressors to improve your blood pressure."

John noticed that Henry and Martha were not expecting that news, and they got worried. He tried to crack a joke: "Oh, come on guys, I've survived a bloody heart attack; I'm sure this sepsis won't affect my health either! Don't worry, I'll be alright soon."

The next day, the hospitalist informed John that his blood cultures came back positive for infection. "Infection from the large intravenous line went into your bloodstream. You have a central line-associated bloodstream infection. We will remove the central line, and I will consult an infectious disease specialist to come and see you."

Sitting in the hospital waiting area, Henry felt a growing uneasiness around him. He was constantly worried about his father's health and trying to get constant updates from the hospital staff.

While sitting there, Henry was recounting memories with his siblings and how close they were as children. Ever since they settled into their professional lives and moved to different places, they couldn't remain in touch as much as they wanted.

A smile appeared on Henry's face as he recalled how they all used to race together on bicycles to go to school, passing through the river and up the mountain to the fields. As the only sister, Cara was always looked after by Michael and Henry. When their parents went somewhere and left them at home, the house was a wrestling ring. He wished they were all there with him, considering what their dad was going through. He was truly missing each one of them at that time, and that void could not be filled.

As he was reminiscing about the good old days, he smiled, remembering how good Michael was at playing guitar. Meanwhile, his sister, Cara, had good vocals and also played piano. Henry himself was good at playing drums. The siblings often dreamt about creating a musical band of their own.

"We are going to be famous!" Henry recalled how Cara would scream these words at the end of every jamming session. Together, they wrote some songs just to perform for their band. These sweet memories brought a much-needed moment of respite amidst the growing tension. At that moment, Henry was jolted back to reality after he heard a knock on the door.

The infectious disease specialist entered the room and introduced himself to John and the other family members. He informed John, "You are getting the correct antibiotics for the type of bacteria that is growing in your blood. You'll need IV antibiotics for several days. We will check your heart to make sure the infection did not spread to the heart."

Martha said, "Doctor, John was progressing well, and we were gearing up for discharge in a day or two. But now he needs a few additional days in the hospital to ensure a full recovery. How did he get this infection in the hospital?"

The doctor explained some of the common reasons why these sorts of infections develop. "It happens when aseptic precautions are not implemented while placing the large intravenous catheter or hygienic interventions like a clean environment, hand hygiene, and sterile techniques while using the catheter are not followed."

"If we don't provide good quality and safe medical care, it can significantly burden patients, families, health systems, and national economy as well. Hospital-acquired conditions like bloodstream infections, falls, pressure ulcers and surgical site infections can increase suffering and mortality in patients. It can result in increased hospital length of stay, readmissions to the hospital and more extensive and expensive medical treatments."

The healthcare costs for these conditions can result in additional financial challenges. That's not just for the patients and the hospital, but also their families because they can lose revenues by spending time away from their work and family members and staying in the hospital. Also, it can be emotionally challenging for the family to see their loved ones suffer.

The doctor continued, "Government ends up spending a significant number of resources as a result of poor-quality care. Rather than spending these valuable resources on improving public health and primary care, implementing innovative programs and other useful interventions, it spends more and more on substandard care."

Henry was curiously listening to the conversation. He had been spending a significant amount of time in the hospital over the past few days. He was missing his wife, Lisa, Sam, and work. The physician turned to Henry and said, "Looks like you have some questions for me. How can I help you?"

Henry replied, "I notice all the staff members regularly using hand sanitizer. I see that the surroundings in the room are clean, and the nurses clean the catheter using alcohol swabs before using it. Dad did not have this infection at the time of admission. How did he still get this infection?"

The physician replied, "I am happy to hear that our staff is implementing best practices to prevent infections in the hospital. Hand hygiene is a very important step in keeping our patients safe. We want our staff to use hand sanitizer before entering and exiting the room, prior to performing any aseptic procedure, and after touching body fluids. We aim to provide the best possible care to our patients by using resources wisely and effectively. In other words, we want to deliver quality medical care to our patients. One of the major principles of medical ethics is to do no harm. We strive to provide safe medical care to our patients."

"I do not have an answer to your question at this time. We will do a drill-down to identify the root cause of this event. We will look for care gaps in the systems, processes or individual errors. If there is a failure in the system or processes, it will have a greater impact than an individual error. We will seek to recognize any patterns, allowing us to detect them early and take proactive steps to prevent similar errors in the future. We will also look for areas where we are doing well and how we can further improve them."

Henry replied, "From my experience staying with my dad in the hospital, I realized how complex the healthcare system is. There are several people involved in taking care of my dad; they are using electronic health records and various technology tools and have different workflows. Mistakes can happen at various levels."

The doctor said, "I agree with you, Henry. The good thing is there is increasing emphasis on improving quality and safety in healthcare. The government has various data reporting programs, and more and more hospital reimbursements are linked to quality and safe medical care rather than the quantity of medical care delivered. Advancements in technology, like artificial intelligence algorithms, can predict adverse events prior to happening. Hospitals are adopting standardized procedures to improve quality and safety."

"Healthcare is a high-reliability organization. We encourage staff to question and report if they notice unsafe practices. We want them to speak up for the safety of our patients. We emphasize the importance of clear communication with each other and with patients and families. Future healthcare professionals are learning about safety and quality improvement during their training. We have checks and balances at various points in the system to prevent mistakes from happening."

Henry asked, "Can we do more to prevent errors from happening?" The doctor answered, "YES!!!"

"I can talk forever on this topic. Let me go and see my other patients. Do you have any questions, John? If not, then I will see you again tomorrow," said the doctor. After a brief pause to ensure John was all set, the doctor gave a reassuring nod and quietly left the room, leaving John and his family to rest and reflect on the conversation.

Henry noticed that Martha was very tired. He knew she would not say it. He said, "Mom, come with me tonight to stay at my place. Lisa was asking about you also."

Martha initially said no but later agreed to go to Henry's house. Henry knew she needed the rest and comfort of home, away from the stressful environment of the hospital.

Henry immediately called Lisa and informed her that Martha was coming with him to stay at their house at tonight.

Henry asked if he should grab something to eat on the way home. He also asked Lisa if she could go to John's place and get Scruffy with her.

Lisa said, "Sam was asking about Scruffy today, too. I will go and get Scruffy to our house tonight. Don't worry about the food—I've already made chicken pasta, so just come straight home. Sam went to bed already but will be happy to see both Martha and Scruffy tomorrow morning."

Martha kissed John on the forehead and said, "Good night, my Love. Have a peaceful sleep."

"Good night, Dad. See you tomorrow," said Henry, and both left the hospital.

Chapter 3

Cara's fingers tapped anxiously on the strap of her bag as she hurriedly gathered her belongings from her cluttered desk. She glanced nervously between the clock's glowing digits and the items she stuffed into her bag. It was already 7 p.m., and the passing time was a harsh reminder of her mounting responsibilities. She was the middle child of Martha and John.

"Honey, I'm so sorry, but I'll be late again," Cara said into the phone, her voice strained with guilt as she waited for the elevator. The distant murmur of conversation echoed in the lobby as she held the phone closer to her ear. "Can you please pick up Daniel from tennis class on your way home?"

On the other end of the line, Steven's tired voice came through, tinged with frustration. "Cara, this is the fourth time this week. I know you're busy, but… I'll pick up Daniel from class, but you need to take care of yourself."

Cara closed her eyes briefly, trying to calm her racing thoughts. "I know, I know. Things have just been so hectic with this big client. But it's important for my career."

The elevator doors opened with a soft ding, and Cara stepped inside, her pulse quickening with each passing second. "Honey, I promise I'll try to be home on time starting tomorrow. Can you please just pick up Daniel from the class? I'll bring food from our favorite Chinese restaurant, so you don't have to cook."

After exchanging strained goodbyes, Cara ended the call, feeling the weight of her choices settle heavily on her shoulders. She knew Steven was right. She was neglecting her health and family for her career, and that realization troubled her conscience.

As the elevator descended, Cara's thoughts drifted to her relentless pursuit of success, a drive that had propelled her from one achievement to the next since childhood. She had always been fiercely competitive and a perfectionist. She excelled in her studies, received top grades, and was skilled in debates and music. She graduated from one of the top business schools in the country, driven by her desire to be the best. Her determination had fueled her rise through school, college, and into the demanding world of finance.

Meeting Steven had been a turning point for Cara. They initially started as colleagues and worked on various projects together. They respected each other's work ethics. Their relationship gradually grew from being colleagues to best friends and eventually to love.

Cara continued to advance in her career. Steven admired her passion for professional growth and encouraged her every step of the way. Steven knew that supporting each other would further strengthen their relationship. They both can reach great heights by helping each other. He never felt overshadowed by her professional success.

When their son Daniel was born, Steven took a more active role in parenting so that Cara could get the needed support at work and home.

Recently, Cara's work commitments have become increasingly demanding, pulling her away from her family more than she would like. With tight deadlines looming and clients placing greater demands on her time, she found herself spending longer hours at the office. While she remains dedicated to her career, the growing time away from home has been weighing on her heart.

Cara felt a sharp pang of guilt as she thought about her distant relationship with her parents, her rare visits, and the rushed phone calls that had become too common. Each missed moment with them reminded her of the sacrifices she had made in her relentless drive for professional success.

She knew her focus on her career had cost her, not just with her parents but in other areas of her life. Despite this, she still believed that these sacrifices were necessary for her career growth and a better future for her family. She hoped that one day, her efforts would help her balance both her personal and professional life without regret.

Lost in her thoughts, Cara nearly missed her stop when the train's brakes screeched loudly. With a muttered curse, she quickly got off the train and made her way through the busy Manhattan streets, her mind full of thoughts about making amends and changing her life.

The smell of takeout filled the air as Cara entered the crowded restaurant. She hurriedly picked up the food and headed back home.

When Cara walked into the apartment, seeing Steven and Daniel made her heartache. Their warm presence was a sharp contrast to the emptiness of her work life. As Daniel hugged her, Cara felt a renewed determination, a quiet promise forming in her mind as she faced her family.

"I'm sorry, you're right. This isn't working anymore. My brain wants me to focus more and more on my job, and my heart wants me to spend more time with my family. I am stuck in between," she said softly but firmly. "I am happy when I am with my family. I think it might be time for me to rethink some things at work or find a better balance."

Steven's smile was kind and understanding as he embraced her. "We just want you home more and to take care of yourself. Family, love, and being together are what really matter, Cara. We miss you."

***

The next morning, Martha and Henry arrived at John's hospital room to visit him. John, usually so positive and cheerful, seemed a bit down today.

"Good morning, Love," Martha said brightly as she and Henry walked in. The sunlight streamed through the window, warming the room. "How are you feeling today? Did you get good sleep last night?"

John sighed, his shoulders drooping with tiredness. "Honestly? Not that great," he admitted.

Martha and Henry exchanged worried glances. The soft hum of medical machines filled the room, mixed with the faint smell of antiseptic. "What's wrong, Dad?" Henry asked.

"I haven't been sleeping well in the hospital. Last night was rough," John explained, looking tired. "I kept getting woken up by all the noises—the beeping machines, people in the hallway, midnight vital sign checks…. I hardly got any sleep."

Martha reached out to adjust the pillows behind John, and her touch was gentle and comforting. "Oh, honey, that sounds awful. I'm so sorry you had such a rough night."

"And when I finally did fall asleep, I had to call for help many times because I needed to use the toilet. I am on a diuretic, and it is making me pass urine several times. But nobody came for a long time. The staff was busy with other patients," John explained.

Pointing to the wires and tubes connected to him, John said "With all this equipment attached to me, I can't get up on my own. I don't want to fall down and worsen my health problems. I don't want a fracture or a head injury and hurt myself more."

Henry nodded sympathetically, his face showing concern. "Well, we're here now, Dad. Is there anything we can do to make you more comfortable?"

John managed a weak smile, his eyes showing gratitude. "I appreciate that. Honestly, I'm just ready to go home. The hospital staff is doing their best, but I'm feeling exhausted. I miss Martha's home-cooked meals. The food here is bland, has less salt, and I could really go for a whole pizza. I'm also feeling weaker."

John brightened a bit as Martha and Henry tried to reassure him. "We'll definitely talk to the charge nurse about this," Martha said, her voice firm. "But first, we want to make sure you're as comfortable as possible while you're here."

Henry added, "And hey, Sam has been asking about you. She's planning to visit in the next day or two if that's okay with you."

John's smile grew at the mention of his granddaughter. "I'd really like that. I miss my little Swifty." John called his granddaughter "Swifty" because she's a big Taylor Swift fan who always plays her music when she visits John and Martha. Sam admires Taylor Swift and considers her as the role model. Her room is filled with photos of Taylor Swift. She likes her persona and how she worked hard to become successful. One day, she wants to attend a Taylor Swift concert. John also started to like Taylor Swift's songs.

Sam lovingly calls John "Big Grandpa." John, who is a bit heavier now, has a jolly presence that fills the room. He used to be quite fit and active while he was young but has gained weight over the years after his children moved out and he cut back on his work.

Just then, a new doctor entered the room. "Good morning, Mr. John. I'm Dr. Jennifer, your hospitalist for the week," she introduced herself, shaking John's hand. She has a warm smile and a friendly demeanor. She pulled up a chair and sat beside his bed.

"How is everything today, Mr. John," asked the doctor.

"Nice to meet you, doctor," John replied, his voice tired but polite. "I was just telling my family I want to go home. I am feeling bored here, not eating well, not getting good sleep. I am becoming physically weak. Am I ready to be discharged?"

Dr. Jennifer said, "Let me update you on your situation." She explained that John's vital signs and lab results looked good, showing that the infection is clearing up.

"However, you need to stay a couple more days to make sure the blood culture stays negative and to have physical therapy and occupational therapy give their recommendations for you to go home. The case manager will check with your health insurance about the plan for intravenous antibiotics after you leave the hospital."

"I know you're eager to leave," Dr. Jennifer said with empathy. "We'll do our best to make the rest of your stay as comfortable as possible. Hang in there, okay?"

John nodded, a glimmer of hope returning to his eyes. "Yes! I'm just counting down the days until I can get back to my home."

The surgeon came to check on John and told him that he was stable enough to be discharged at any time from his standpoint. The infectious disease doctor came in and gave a different update. "Mr. John, I think we can get you discharged in two days."

The nurse came to dispense medicines to John. John asked the nurse about his discharge plan as well. She said, "I am not sure when you are getting out of the hospital. I will ask the case manager to come and talk with you."

Henry and Martha exchanged a puzzled glance, sensing the mixed messages. Henry said. "Is there a plan to coordinate your care?"

The nurse paused—her brow furrowed in thought. "Hmm, let me circle back with the hospitalist. We'll make sure we're all on the same page about your timeline for discharge."

John sighed heavily—frustration evident in his tired voice. "I'm just getting really confused and frustrated with all these different updates."

Martha squeezed John's hand reassuringly. "I'm going to talk to the charge nurse about improving communication between the team members. You shouldn't have to be the one piecing it all together."

Just then, Henry's phone rang. It was his sister, Cara, who face-timed from New York. "Hey Cara, I was just thinking about you."

Henry proceeded to fill Cara in on all the details of John's medical situation. "OMG, I thought he was improving well after the medical emergency and the surgery. I had no idea dad was going through all these additional medical issues.

Unfortunately, I haven't been able to visit him. This major client has been very demanding, and the pressure at work with important assignments has kept me tied up. It's been a bit overwhelming. I'm coming there to see Dad," she said, her voice thick with emotion.

After confirming the latest flight out of New York, Cara promised Henry she'd be there as soon as possible with her family. But then she remembered, "Are Michael and Ashley coming in from Los Angeles to be with dad, too? They should know what's happening."

A glower crossed Henry's face. "I left him a message, but you know how he is about returning calls. I hope he listens to my voicemail and calls me back. He has not been in touch with any of us for a long time." Cara rolled her eyes, frustration evident in her expression. But this wasn't the time to indulge old grudges.

True to form, Michael didn't reply before Cara's flight took off. She touched down along with her family, exhausted, to find Henry waiting as promised. In the car, she asked again about Michael and Ashley.

Henry sighed. "Voicemail, but there's no answer."

Cara remained silent, her heart heavy with worry. Some things never changed, no matter how far she moved away. All she could do now was focus on being there for Dad during his recovery, just like they always had when they were children. The past could wait—loving their father was the only thing that truly mattered.

Cara gazed out the hospital window, lost in memories of simpler days. She and Michael's wife, Ashley, had been so close once, as neighbors and classmates since preschool.

They had sleepovers, giggled late into the night, and shared their hopes and dreams. They were best friends.

It was Cara who first encouraged Ashley: "You should talk to Michael—I know he's nice." Little did she know it would lead to problems that later strained their friendship.

In high school, Ashley began to shine. She joined the cheer squad and always had lead roles in plays. Cara, who always wanted to be the best, felt overshadowed by Ashley's growing popularity. Jealousy, ego, and insecurity took root without her realizing it.

Their bond weakened as Ashley's social circle grew while Cara focused on studying hard to escape their small-town life. She watched from the sidelines as Ashley and Michael became close, rehearsing for school musicals.

The final blow came when Ashley and Michael decided to move to Los Angeles to pursue studies in the arts. Cara criticized Michael, saying he was being irresponsible and would never succeed. She wanted him to stay, finish undergrad, and get into a good graduate program. Michael's decision to follow Ashley across the country instead of staying with his family hurt Cara deeply.

Their falling out left deep wounds that never truly healed. Over the years, tense encounters during Cara's visits home only added to the bitterness. Now, under these difficult circumstances, old issues resurfaced despite her efforts to move past them.

When Cara entered the room with Steven and Daniel, her father's face lit up, seeing his beloved family. "There's my girl Cara, Steven, and my handsome nugget Daniel!" John said with a weak but genuine smile.

Cara leaned down to hug him gently. "We came as soon as we could, Dad. How are you feeling?" She gripped his hand, giving it a comforting squeeze.

John's cheeks were regaining color, and he was surrounded by those he loved. Having his family around made a big difference for John. While his medical condition might be slowly improving, the presence of family brought a sense of recovery that no medical treatment could provide.

Having more family members around and words of encouragement from his friends made John and Martha realize that they were not alone in this medical journey.

John agreed to stay in the hospital until he was ready for discharge. Laughter and memories filled the room with warmth and light.

***

The next morning, John was resting in his room when the chaplain came in to introduce himself. "Good morning, Mr. John. I am one of the chaplains at this hospital. I heard from nursing that you've been through a lot. Is there anything I can do for you?"

John replied, "No, I am feeling much better now that my family has returned from New York."

"That's excellent. Is it OK if I talk with you about advanced care planning?"

John looked a bit hesitant. "Advanced care planning? I've never heard of that before. What does that mean exactly?"

"Well, it's about making sure your medical care preferences and wishes are clearly documented, especially for times when you might not be able to speak for yourself," the chaplain explained.

He continued, "We'll talk about the kind of care you would want. Things like whether you'd want life support, nutrition through tubes if needed, your wishes for end-of-life care, and who you'd want to make decisions for you."

John frowned. "That sounds kind of heavy. I mean, I'm not planning on dying anytime soon."

The chaplain nodded kindly. "I know it's not the easiest thing to think about. However, situations can arise where you might not be able to make your own medical choices. Advanced care planning helps ensure your wishes are followed instead of leaving it up to your loved ones to guess."

He added, "It's about being proactive and having a plan in place ahead of time so you're not just reacting to an emergency. You can always update things if your situation or preferences change."

John paused. "So, how do I start figuring out what I would want in those situations?"

"Great question," the chaplain replied. "Start by thinking about your main values and priorities in life. What matters to you the most? What kind of quality of life do you want? These can guide your decisions." He encouraged John to discuss it with his family, too.

"I understand it's not easy, but being proactive can really help take the burden off your loved ones later. It can be emotionally challenging for them to make tough decisions during emergencies. They'll know they're honoring your wishes instead of facing difficult choices," the chaplain said.

He offered to support John through the process and then left. John felt a mix of emotions, feeling a bit speechless.

The next morning, John seemed quieter. "There's no need to worry about all that end-of-life paperwork," he said bluntly when Cara brought it up. "I'm doing just fine, so let's change the subject."

Cara tried gently to influence him. "Dad, it's okay to prepare," but John cut her off. "No more talk of that. Enough, Cara! Let's cheer up for Henry's sake." He winked at Henry, who smiled in return.

That evening, the family arranged a small dinner in John's room to celebrate his progress. Laughter filled the room as they shared stories over paper plates.

The only thing that cast a shadow over their spirits was Michael's absence—he still hadn't returned calls or come to visit. And at home, John's loyal dog, Scruffy, missed his best friend.

"Scruffy must be missing Dad," Cara said sadly. The old dog had been John's constant companion for over a decade.

Henry agreed. "I wish we could bring Scruffy here, but you know the hospital rules. No pets are allowed unless they're certified therapy animals."

As the charge nurse made her daily rounds, they updated her on John's improved condition. "We're so grateful for everything you and the staff have done," Henry said warmly. But he also admitted their frustration with poorly coordinated updates that weren't always in sync.

"It's like an orchestra where all the musicians have their part, but they aren't performing as one unit to deliver captivating music," Henry said. Martha also shared John's concerns about lack of sleep and bland food with the charge nurse.

Henry added, "Dad is alive today because of the medical staff's dedication. But all the great work isn't always translating into improved patient satisfaction."

The charge nurse listened to their concerns, expressed empathy, and apologized for the care gaps. She explained recent steps to improve care coordination, like having the healthcare team round daily as a team to improve communication and share insights so patients and their caregivers get consistent information.

She also addressed John's other complaints. She explained the rationale for low-salt food. She informed them that John could build fluid easily in his body if he ate more salty food. This can result in more shortness of breath and swelling of his legs and abdomen. She also assured them that they would take measures to ensure John gets uninterrupted sleep at nighttime.

She added, "Improving patient satisfaction is one of the top priorities in healthcare. There are patient satisfaction surveys and star ratings."

"Effective communication is crucial for patient satisfaction. We encourage our staff to use techniques like the 'teach-back method,' where we ask patients to repeat what they understand about their health. Other methods, like 'bedside reports' during shift changes, can also help improve communication."

"In addition to keeping communication open, we also focus on sharing information regularly with patients. We want to involve patients and their families in their medical care and get their feedback to build strong and respectful partnerships. Basically, we're all about making care patient-and-family-centered," the charge nurse explained.

As their discussion came to a close, Martha said, "I hope this approach helps ease fears and doubts during what can be really tough medical situations."

Henry added, "Clear communication is key. It helps patients and families feel much more at ease."

The charge nurse also added, "Improving employee satisfaction often leads to better patient and caregiver satisfaction. However, with the current healthcare shortages, staff are working hard, and it's still a work in progress."

Henry thanked the charge nurse for understanding their concerns and for the care provided. He appreciated the effort the staff put in despite the challenging conditions. "It's no wonder burnout is so common in this field," he said.

The charge nurse offered to have a patient representative come and discuss their concerns further. As she was about to leave, her phone alerted her to a rapid response from another patient. With a quick apology, she hurried off.

Watching her leave, Henry wondered, "Do you think technology might help ease the workload in the future?

Maybe robots could handle repetitive tasks, or artificial intelligence could help with things like accurate radiology image interpretation, predicting patient deterioration from medical conditions like sepsis, providing support in diagnosis and management of diseases, and medical billing and coding."

Cara agreed that innovations could be promising if they support, rather than replace, caregivers. "The human touch is irreplaceable. But if technology can free up time by handling things like documentation, it could make a big difference." It is also important to watch for issues like health data privacy and security and prevent biases while building these artificial intelligence algorithms.

As they wrapped up their conversation, the family felt more connected and hopeful about John's care. While there were still challenges ahead, they felt reassured by the focus on coordinated care, open communication, and the potential benefits of technology in healthcare.

Chapter 4

While John was still in the hospital, he got a wonderful surprise. Sam came to visit her beloved Grandpa. John's face lit up with joy when he saw Swifty, who was just as excited to meet him.

Sam hurried to John's bedside, giving him a big hug and a kiss. "I'm so glad you're feeling better, Big Grandpa!" she said with a smile. Just having family around lifted John's spirits.

Martha took Sam to the waiting room, where she was thrilled to see her aunt Cara. Even though it had been a few years since they last met in person, their bond was still strong. Cara greeted Sam with a warm hug, delighted to see her.

Sam was equally happy to see her Uncle Steven. After such a long time apart, the reunion was full of joy and affection. The whole room was brightened by their smiles.

When Sam spotted her cousin, Daniel, she ran over and hugged him tightly. "Daniel, I'm so glad to see you!" she exclaimed. Despite the years that had passed, she fondly remembered her playful cousin.

Daniel grinned and reminisced, "I remember when we used to play on Grandpa's porch swings." He talked about the fun summer days they had spent on the farm, running through the cornfields and picking fresh corn for barbecues.

Even though John was feeling weak, his smile grew wider hearing the joyful chatter. His pain and fatigue seemed a little lighter with Sam's laughter and warm presence.

Sam noticed how frail John looked and teasingly said, "Grandpa, did they forget to feed you in here?" John chuckled and explained that he hadn't had much energy lately.

To pass the time in the hospital, John listened to music on his phone. "That Taylor Swift song you suggested has really stuck in my head," he joked. They bonded over their shared love for her music.

When John tried to get up to show Sam his playlist, his weak body faltered. Sam quickly fetched the phone, and they scrolled through his music together, stopping on songs that brought back happy memories.

One song reminded Sam of past Thanksgiving and missing John's pumpkin pie this year because of his hospital stay. "Don't worry, I'll bake you the best pie for next

Thanksgiving," John promised. Sam couldn't wait, knowing her grandpa's pie recipe was unbeatable.

Later, the physical and occupational therapists came to check on John. They had him walk in the hallways, climb stairs, and assess his balance. They determined that John was quite weak and suggested a stay at a nursing home for more intensive therapy.

The hospitalist visited and explained, "The therapists recommend a short stay at the nursing home. With your motivation, we think two to three weeks of therapy should help you regain significant strength and independence." The hospitalist assured John that this was the best way to get back to full health.

John was not eager to go to the nursing home, but eventually, he agreed. Though he was recovering steadily, he knew he was weaker from his lengthy hospital stay. His mobility was impacted by a lack of regular physical activity. He was getting very tired quickly, even when walking short distances without help down the hallway.

Before this, he had no problem with even climbing stairs. He didn't want Martha to get sick since she had been with him throughout this health care ordeal. He knew she was getting weak and tired, and her well-being was just as important as his own.

"Honey, caring for you is the easiest thing after all these things," Martha said. Though John was getting better, deep down, she knew he needed an intense exercise program to fully regain his strength and coordination.

"The doctor said it was only for a short stay at the nursing home. After the rehabilitation, I will be much stronger. I will be dancing jigs in no time," John said.

Sam looked at Grandma Martha and said gratefully, "Mom told me you've been so caring to Grandpa through all this. You love him a lot."

A soft smile spread on Martha's face. Sam asked Martha how it all began, hoping to lift their spirits with a sweet memory from the past.

John told Sam to hand over his wallet. He took out a photo of him and Martha together, which was taken several decades ago during their trip to Yellowstone National Park near the Roosevelt Arch.

Martha's eyes shone, remembering as if it were yesterday. "My girlfriends and I decided to go to the Black Hills to visit Mount Rushmore; at the same time, your grandpa went with some buddies. We roared through the black hills on our motorcycles, stopping to gas up along the way. As I removed my helmet, shaking out my long hair, I noticed the most handsome man across the way. Your grandpa was filling his car at the same pump, tall and easy-smiling. When our eyes met, I felt a spark. His warm gaze made my heart flutter."

She sighed, continuing. "I couldn't get those kind brown eyes out of my mind the whole trip. After we returned home, I often thought back to the man from the Mount Rushmore trip and wondered if our paths would cross again. Little did I know how that meeting by chance would change my life forever," she told Sam.

"Over time, John and I reunited in the most unexpected of ways. Our chance encounter blossomed into a deep love that has lasted ever since. It was true love at first sight," she added.

"That's when things really started getting exciting in our love story!" Martha continued. "A few months later, John and I both decided to take a trip to Yellowstone National Park, though separately with friends again. As fate would have it, we all stopped at the same roadside restaurant for lunch."

A smile appeared on her face as she recalled the good old days.

"You can imagine our surprise when John and I ended up sitting at tables right next to each other! I could barely eat— my stomach was in such knots, noticing him there. Out of the corner of my eye, I watched John fidget too. Finally, he gathered the courage to introduce himself," Martha shared how the two felt at that moment.

"We hit it off right away, chatting easily about where we were from and our travels so far. John had the warmest smile, which just melted me. Before long, we had completely lost track of time, too caught up in our conversations to eat. Our friends had to practically drag us away when it was time to leave, reluctantly saying 'goodbye' once more."

There was a brief silence in the room as everyone was keenly looking at Martha to share what happened next.

"But that chance encounter at the restaurant lit a fire in our hearts. I knew then there was something truly special between John and me, and I hoped this wouldn't be the last I saw of him." Martha continued telling Sam the tale with a faraway look. "And would you believe, by some miracle, we crossed paths yet again! This time, we were both staying at the same lodge, near Old Faithful Geyser, of course."

"As John and I passed each other in the lobby, we couldn't believe our eyes. We immediately ditched our groups to catch up, knowing this was no mere coincidence. At that point, it was clear that the chemistry between us was undeniable," Martha shared.

"Our friends quickly saw the spark, too. Our whole crew bonded over the next few days while exploring the park together. I had never laughed or felt as comfortable with anyone as I did with John by my side. We stayed up each night for hours talking by the fire, learning every detail of each other's lives."

"What started as separate trips soon became a shared adventure," Martha continued dreamily. "For the rest of that magical week, our groups stuck together, exploring every corner of Yellowstone. John and I took it all in, with the ever-changing travertine terraces of Mammoth hot springs, the rainbow of hot pools at Norris, and artistic views alongside Mystic Falls."

"We hiked for hours at a time but barely got tired, too enraptured in each other's company to notice. Day after day passed in a blissful haze, discovering nature's grandest sights: the thundering Grand Canyon of Yellowstone, herds of bison on the plains, and bears fishing in the blue lakes.

Every moment with John left me feeling like the luckiest woman alive.

We capped off each perfect day with big group dinners and campfire parties deep into the night. I felt completely at peace by John's side, taking in the boundless beauty of Yellowstone and the blossoming beauty of our connection. Before we knew it, a week had flown by in what seemed like mere hours together. Neither of us was ready to say goodbye."

Martha's eyes shone brightly, recalling that magical time.

"When the week came to a close, neither John nor I wanted it to end. We had become inseparable over those few short days. But sadly, it was time for our friends to depart for home. As they packed up to go, John looked at me with a question in his eyes. 'Martha, would you... maybe want to stay on a bit longer?' he asked tentatively. 'I'm not ready to leave Yellowstone or...or you just yet.'"

She paused, tearing up a bit.

"My heart soared hearing him say the words I desperately wanted to. *Nothing would make me happier, John, I beamed.* And so, at that moment, we made the spontaneous decision to remain in each other's company, if only for a little while longer. Our friends wished us well as they left, already understanding what was blossoming between us," Martha added.

"For the next glorious week, it was just John and I exploring the park together, side by side. This time, we had each other all to ourselves, and our relationship only continued to deepen with every passing moment."

Martha let out a dreamy sigh at the memory. "That next week with John flew by even faster than the first. We decided to take my motorcycle and extend our adventure, heading over to the Grand Tetons. Whizzing through those scenic highways with John wrapped close behind me. I had never felt so alive and free. In Grand Teton, we were like lovebirds, inseparable as we explored every hidden corner of that equally stunning park. We camped under starry mountain skies along Jackson Lake, waking to swim in its crystal waters with the jagged peaks as our backdrop. Hiking together along Jenny Lake or strolling Inspiration Point with John's hand in mine made every panoramic vista of nature's splendor seem that much more inspiring."

"But most breathtaking of all was the way he looked at me as if I were more beautiful than any grand landscape. By then, I knew in my heart that this wonderful man was destined to be a permanent part of my life's journey from that day onwards."

"Ah, Glacier National Park! That magical week holds some of my fondest memories with John," Martha recalled warmly. "Riding my bike along the Going-to-the-Sun Road with him wrapped behind me, taking in those stunning Sierra vistas at every curve, was pure bliss. We felt like we were floating on air above it all."

"At Logan Pass, strolling through breathtaking meadows and waterfalls under such a big sky, it felt as if John and I had journeyed to our own personal heaven on earth. The hike to Hidden Lake Overlook was especially romantic. Stealing kisses with that crystal blue lake and mountainous backdrop will forever remain etched in my heart."

"By the end of our incredible trip together, it truly did feel as though John and I had known each other for years, not weeks. Through long talks by the campfire while stargazing, we covered every facet of each other's lives—our families, dreams, memories, everything! John was so easy to confide in, and in turn, I felt I knew his soul."

"Leaving each other at the end, neither of us wanted to say goodbye. But I like to think it was 'see you later,' as our love story was only just beginning."

Martha sighed blissfully as she reflected on that transformative summer. "When we finally parted ways after that unforgettable trip, John and I kept our love strong through long letters, planning to see each other again soon."

And the next time John came to visit me, he asked if he could meet my parents too. I'll never forget the look of adoration in his eyes as he expressed his deep love and intentions towards me. My mama and papa liked John right away as well. They were quite impressed by how devoted he was to making me happy.

With their blessing and support, John continued courting me throughout the following year. We took a few more trips together, cementing our tight bond. When the time was finally right, John asked for my hand in the marriage. And so, after much joyous planning with our families, we wed the next spring in a beautiful outdoor ceremony, surrounded by those we loved most.

John and I went on to build a beautiful life together based on that foundation of care, trust, and understanding established during that magical Yellowstone summer that brought us together all those years ago."

As Martha finished sharing their chance meeting, Sam smiled, heartened by their deep love. "You two give me hope for finding a deep love like that someday."

Martha patted her hand warmly. "You'll know it's right when someone chooses to see you, respect your dignity, and uphold you every single day through all of life's ups and downs with kindness, empathy, and unwavering commitment."

Other family members were also immersed in the conversation. "Tell me more, Mom. What has made you both love each other for so many decades?" Cara asked.

Martha smiled warmly. "Of course, darling. For instance, your dad knows my hip's been bothering me more lately. So, without saying a word, he takes my arm every time we go up and down the stairs together."

"Aw, that's so sweet," Cara remarked.

Martha nodded. "It is. And I know caffeine makes his acid reflux worse, but he still gives me company each morning because it's our time to chat."

Thinking back, Martha added, "When we hit a rough patch after you were born, work was stressful for both of us. But your dad made sure to rub my feet each night without failing. It was his quiet way of showing he still cared deeply."

Cara listened intently, soaking in these small acts of consideration. "Being married isn't just about the big romantic gestures," Martha continued. "It's showing through little daily things that you're still committed to the other person's well-being and happiness. The trust between them keeps the love going," Cara smiled, feeling grateful for this wisdom from her mom.

John smiled softly, gazing at Martha with deep admiration. "From the moment I first laid eyes on your mom, I knew she was something special. But it was her inner strength that truly made me fall."

"That woman has been the rock holding this family together through everything. Even back then, she had a fiery spirit and wise heart well beyond her years." Sam listened intently as John reminisced.

"As soon as we started dating, storms would come blowing in, but your grandma was always calm in the center. Not a thing in this world seems to shake that woman or make her lose her head." John shook his head in playful disbelief.

"I remember one time, the roof nearly caved in during a bad hailstorm. But Martha just boarded up the leaks and cooked us the best chicken stew, like it was any old day. That's when I knew nobody else could ever be my partner and support through this life."

Martha had drifted over to John's bedside as he spoke, affection shining on her face. "He always did have a way of over-exaggerating my abilities—bless his heart," she said warmly, giving John's arm an affectionate pat.

Cara grasped both their hands. "You sure did pick a good one, Dad. I can see why that deep understanding you two have developed has lasted you so long. I'm grateful every day for the example you both have been for us." They shared smiles, taking comfort in facing life's challenges together as a united front.

The case manager came to talk with the family regarding nursing home options. "John, I know you are ready to leave the hospital. However, some arrangements still need to be sorted out before you can be discharged from the hospital," she informed them of the prior authorization process with the insurance company.

"They will review your case and decide if physical therapy and intravenous antibiotics at the nursing home are medically necessary. If they are denied, we will discuss alternate treatment options or out-of-pocket expenses. This process can take some time. In the meantime, I will call different nursing homes to check on the availability of beds," she added.

John requested the case manager to find a nursing home closer to his residence so that Martha, Henry, and their friends wouldn't have to drive long distances to visit him.

"Nowadays, it is becoming hard to find beds with openings at nursing homes. Our population is aging, and many nursing homes have limited space and are filled with other patients. There is a shortage of trained medical staff at nursing homes. Regulatory challenges and insufficient reimbursements are also resulting in more shortages of nursing home beds. The weekend is coming up. We must wait at least till Monday to get these answers. Once I hear from them, I will come back and update you," the case manager said.

Cara's family decided to go back to New York, knowing John was medically stable and waiting for nursing home placement. Cara and Steven said their 'goodbyes' to John. Sam turned to her cousin, Daniel. "I'm really going to miss you, Daniel!" she said, mussing his hair playfully. Daniel gave her a long hug, not wanting to let go.

"You'll have to come visit me in New York soon. I will show you tall buildings and museums. I will take you to my school and the tennis courts. We can eat food at different restaurants," he told Sam earnestly. She smiled, promising to make the trip. For now, John's recovery is the family's top priority.

Exchanging one last wave as Cara's car pulled away, the whole family felt sad at saying 'goodbye' for an unknown time. But they took comfort in knowing they were supporting each other through this long distance, just as they rallied around John.

John sighed, already missing his daughter, son-in-law, and grandson. But he felt strengthened knowing his loved ones remained in each other's lives during this challenge. He knew progress took different forms at different stages. Determination kept John's spirits up through any issues. He hopes to be energized to new heights again soon.

The nurse made a game of physiotherapy exercises for John to play over the weekend. She cheered John on while he did his exercises. "Look at you, go! You'll be dancing with Martha in no time at this rate!" Her appreciation kept his confidence going.

The case manager came back on Monday afternoon to update the family. "I am still waiting for the insurance's prior authorization approval. They asked for more paperwork. I faxed them," she informed them.

John grew frustrated. Martha noticed it and said, "I know it's hard waiting, dear. The case manager is working on it."

The case manager told them, "Insurance companies want to prevent fraud and misuse and control their costs through this process. It can be time-consuming at times, increasing the length of hospital stays for patients. Uniform prior authorization requirements for all insurance companies can simplify this process. Tools like electronic prior authorization systems, their integration with electronic health records, and using predictive analytics for less complex cases can save time."

John sighed. "With each day, I am losing movement. I feel my strength gradually fading. What if I can't dance with you again?" Martha held his hand reassuringly. "Don't you fret; we'll get through this."

"Thank you all for never giving up on me. With your love and care, I know I'll recover stronger than ever."

Henry did his best to keep his spirits up during this delay. He brought him news and treats from home. He knew that hearing news about Sam would lift John's spirits. Friends of John and Martha have been calling and visiting them in the hospital to provide support.

The next day, case manager brought the good news. "Finally, you are approved by the insurance company to go to the nursing home. The nursing home closer to your residence has no beds today, but they informed me there's a bed opening tomorrow. They'll get you back on your feet in no time. I will request the hospitalist to enter discharge orders tomorrow morning. I will arrange a ride for tomorrow," she informed them with a smile.

John, Martha, and Henry were happy listening to the case manager.

The next day, John was discharged with instructions to continue his recovery at the nursing home. Martha and Henry helped dress him in comfortable clothes, and a nurse's assistant arrived to transport John by wheelchair to the awaiting ambulance. Martha kissed John's forehead. "I'll see you at the nursing home," she reassured.

***

The nursing home was housed in a large, old home that had been converted for its purposes. The wide corridors and abundance of tall windows throughout let in plenty of natural light. Upon entry, there was a spacious front parlor area with comfortable seating.

The resident rooms were arranged in long hallways on each floor. John's room was a modest, midsized space with a private bathroom and enough space for a couch and chair so Martha could stay overnight if needed. Nursing stations were centrally located for easy monitoring. There was a large activity area with craft supplies, books, and board games. Residents socialize here on most afternoons.

The dining room was open and bright, with seating staggered over mealtimes. Nutritious meals were prepared fresh daily in the on-site kitchen. Overall, the facility offered a comforting environment for recovery.

After getting settled in his room, John slept fitfully for much of that first afternoon and night. The whirring of equipment and the beeps of monitors were a constant reminder of why he was there.

John took in his new surroundings at the nursing home with some nervousness. Though he'd longed to start recovery, John felt anxious at the change. The room felt sterile compared to the home's warmth. Martha saw his hesitation and said, "I am here for you, my love. We will do it together."

After a pause, John nodded slowly. As much as he feared the transition, he knew physically that this was the best step. "Alright...for our future dances together, I'll give it my all here."

"Big things are ahead during your new phase of recovery. You're so strong. I know you'll do wonderfully here," said Henry.

Martha made John's room feel cozy with photos and little touches from home.

The caring staff at the nursing home made an excellent first impression, getting John situated and starting treatment right away. "It may not look like much now, but just wait. This place will help you gain your stride in no time!" said his lively physical therapist. John smiled weakly, wanting to believe her optimism.

The first few days dragged on as John got used to the new place. But soon, a friendly neighbor in the next room struck up a conversation. "It gets easier, you'll see. Just take it one step at a time," the neighbor encouraged with a smile.

At first, even small tasks left him winded. Meals were hard work for John, as his energy ran out easily. He could only eat small portions now when he usually ate hearty, big meals. The tiredness was clear on his face. He had bags under his eyes from being exhausted.

Physiotherapy and occupational therapy sessions helped John each day. Physically, the activities challenged him, yet each small achievement boosted his spirit. Before he knew it, John looked forward to the purr of activity rather than fearing the long days lying in hospital beds. Slowly, walking the halls grew easier, though tiring. Calls from Cara and his family rallied his morale, too.

By the end of John's first week, John continued to improve under the medical staff's devoted care. His strength and appetite gradually returned. His smiles came easier and more frequent, seeing Martha's beaming pride at each gain. Each milestone, be it a flight of stairs or an extra helping at meals, drove John's vigor higher.

Knowing his dad was settled at the nursing home, Henry decided to go back to work. When John was in the hospital for several days, he stayed by his side around the clock. But the bills didn't stop, so he knew he must return to work.

"Don't you worry, Dad, I'll be back whenever I get a chance. You keep working hard and recovering fast so I can take you fishing soon, yeah?" John patted his arm. "You've been the best son I could ask for. Now get on to work so I know things are taken care of."

Luckily, Henry's boss was quite understanding of the family emergency that was keeping Henry absent. "Just focus on your dad getting better. Take all the time you need—your job will be here." Henry was grateful for the flexibility in such a stressful season.

In Henry's absence, Lisa was taking care of the family and Sam. She understood that John and Martha needed Henry's support during these testing times.

Martha was tired from John's health care journey. But she was always there for John's every need. "You rest, dear. I can manage here awhile," John would insist tenderly.

But Martha would have none of it. "Wherever you go, I'll go too. That's what we promised all those years ago."

Best of all, like clockwork, Martha arrived daily with updates to lift his mood. "You're thriving, my love! Soon, you'll be back in my arms, where you belong. For now, just focus on you." John felt deeply grateful for this phase and all the support that enabled his recovery.

One day, Martha brought a special guest, Scruffy. Nursing homes allow pets. "Look who's here to see you!"

Martha said, letting Scruffy's leash go. He bounded over, nearly tackling John with eager licks and whimpers. Martha had tears in her eyes seeing John's pure joy reunited with his furry buddy.

A few days later, a worrying envelope was addressed to John. Inside were medical bills from his medical ordeal. His medical insurance only covered a part of the expenses.

John sighed heavily, his heart sinking at the figure. But ever-resilient Martha said, "Don't you worry, we'll manage this like everything else."

Seeing John's spirits fall, she gently said, "Remember, dear, what's most important is that you're here, regaining your strength each day with those who love you. Don't let these bills undermine all your progress. Just keep focusing on you," John nodded, reassured.

As usual, a social worker at the nursing home came on rounds to check on the residents. When she stopped by John's room, she noticed his worried brow. She asked gently, "What's troubling you, John?" John sighed, showing her the medical bills.

The social worker continued her conversation by asking sensitive yet important questions.

"How are you adjusting financially to healthcare costs, John? Is there enough support at home?" She understood how factors like education, income, housing, food access, understanding of health conditions, and transportation influenced well-being.

Social determinants of health were really the root of health inequity. Things like where one was born, grows up, lives, and works could influence one's health. These scenarios could be out of one's control.

The social worker wanted to ensure John's recovery wasn't delayed by worries outside of clinical care. She wanted John to fully focus on physical and mental healing. In this situation, a holistic approach was so important for regaining health and hope. They agreed to explore resources if bills felt too burdensome. This conversation relieved his stress, if only temporarily.

The next day, the social worker came back with some financial aid resources. Just then, Henry came to visit his dad. "Hello, Dad. How are the exercises going? Are you building more muscles? How are the six packs coming along?" he joked. John was typically a pleasant guy. But he was experiencing a slump that day.

Henry turned to the social worker and asked what the matter was. The social worker informed him about their conversation regarding expensive medical bills.

Henry started looking at medical bills as well. "I thought Dad had good medical insurance. But I see he needs to pay a significant amount of money. Why is health care so expensive?"

The social worker empathized with them. Medical debt is one of the leading causes of personal bankruptcy in America.

She went on to add, "There are many factors driving higher costs. Labor and capital costs are expensive. There is a lack of price regulation and price transparency. Our healthcare system is complex and extremely fragmented, resulting in high administrative costs."

"Since malpractice bills are costly, we practice defensive medicine and sometimes order diagnostic tests and sophisticated imaging, which can be expensive. As we all know, prescription medications are also costly."

"Preventative care is underfunded compared to expensive acute care in the hospitals. A big chunk of money is spent on inpatient care and emergency department visits for non-emergent medical conditions. A substantial amount of health care resources are utilized during the last year of the patient's life," she added.

The two discussed a few potential solutions for this overwhelming challenge. Focusing on primary care, preventive medicine, and value-based payment models may help reduce the costs. Technology tools like electronic health records and artificial intelligence can help improve communication between various parties in health care and reduce administrative costs. Promote price transparency and negotiate drug prices with pharmacy companies. The government must prioritize programs targeted at improving social determinants of health, community outreach programs, and healthy lifestyles through public and private partnerships.

Another crucial topic is the strategies to expand health care coverage to the population and ways to simplify the health care regulatory landscape.

"Though daunting, having a conversation through open dialogue and united voices is the first step towards positive change," the social worker said.

Henry listened carefully, grateful for her insights, yet overwhelmed by such a challenging systemic problem. His dad didn't deserve more worries through it all.

Recognizing Henry's concern, the social worker reassured him, "You folks don't need to shoulder this burden alone. We'll do our best to alleviate financial strain from these bills."

That evening, Henry called Cara to discuss the medical bills and how stressed John and Martha were from the bills. "The social worker is helping to sort it out, but what they've endured to get well isn't right," he said.

John and Martha's church community has already come forward to provide support, but the medical bills are so high, and they need additional help to cover the costs.

Cara felt bad. "I'll look into more assistance programs they qualify for and create a fundraiser to generate additional funds to support them during this challenging time. Our community always comes through for each other."

She knew John and Martha didn't have as much money saved up. Cara told Henry, "Don't worry, I want to help. We will see how much money we can generate through the fundraiser. I will make plans to pay the remaining medical bills for Dad."

Henry was so grateful. He knew this would lift a huge weight off of John and Martha. When he told them of Cara's offer, they couldn't believe it. Happy tears started rolling from Martha's eyes because Cara's help took away their biggest concern.

Now, John could put all his energy into physical therapy at the nursing home. He would start to feel better knowing his family was taking care of everything. This allowed him to have peace of mind during his recovery. That was the power of family and community coming together during difficult times.

Chapter 5

Martha sighed happily as she looked around the living room and dining area of the nursing home. The staff had really outdone themselves with decorations for the holidays. Garlands of holly and ribbons lined the fireplace mantel and every doorway. A towering Christmas tree in the corner of the living room was strung with twinkling lights and shiny baubles.

"It sure looked festive in here, didn't it, love?" Martha said, taking John's hand. He smiled wearily from his armchair. His physical strength and coordination had improved significantly, and he also completed the course of intravenous antibiotics.

"Nothing like being with family to celebrate Christmas," John nodded. "Even if our family couldn't be here, at least we still had each other." He patted Martha's hand softly.

Martha agreed and said, "I know you miss the comforts of home, dear," she said softly. "It's so natural to want your own bed and TV again after so long. The doctor said you are almost ready to go home."

"The food's not bad, but it's no match for your roast chicken on Christmas either!" John managed a small smile, though his eyes remained sad. He preferred to spend Christmas at his sweet home.

Martha sighed. "I wished more than anything we could be back in our house together. But this is only temporary, so think of all the progress you've made thanks to the therapy here. Before we know it, you'll be all well. You've got a long life ahead of you, John. Christmas will come around again next year, and many more, God willing. You focus on getting your strength back so you can watch all the TV you like."

Just then, the physical therapist came to perform exercises with John. The physical therapist was impressed with his overall progress. From a therapy standpoint, I can let you go home with an exercise regimen to practice at home.

The physician examined John as well. "You're one of our success stories, Mr. John. It warms our hearts to see the progress you've made thanks to your hard work and support system. You improved faster than we anticipated. I can discharge you from here. You can spend Christmas at home with friends and family.

The ejection fraction, or pumping of your heart, is reduced because of the heart attack. You must take your medicines regularly. Check your weight daily. Eat a low-salt diet so that you don't build up fluid in your body. Great work, John," the physician said.

Martha called Henry and informed him about the good news. He asked if they needed any help with packing and ride back home. Martha and John were grateful for Henry's unconditional support throughout this healthcare journey. "You focus on your work and family, son. We will catch up later at our house," John said.

The smile on John's face was brighter than ever as he watched Martha pack the last of his things in the nursing home. "I can hardly believe that finally, I'm leaving to go home."

Martha beamed at him. "You've come so far, my love. It seems like just yesterday you could barely walk through those doors."

John's neighbor at the nursing home wheeled over. "I'll sure miss having you around, but this calls for a celebration! What do you say we go out to lunch later, my treat?" John agreed happily.

As John and Martha prepared to leave, the nurse came to wish him well and expressed how much she had enjoyed caring for him. "I just want to make sure you have all the information you need at home," she said kindly. "Your progress has been excellent, but keeping up with medications is crucial to staying healthy."

She went over the discharge instructions. She reviewed each prescription in detail. Dosage, timing, and potential side effects. "I know it's a little complicated but follow the plan closely. And if you have any questions or concerns, please call us."

John nodded and repeated the discharge instructions. Staying on track would ensure he didn't end up back in the hospital. Martha added the instructions to their daily routine calendar as a backup.

"If you are not feeling well, then call us right away, understand?" the nurse emphasized. John promised he would.

Finally, hugs were shared all around. "Our doors are always open if you need us. But I have a feeling you'll do just great at home with your wonderful support," the social worker smiled.

As they drove off, John felt grateful not just to the staff but also for the people in his life who cared for him. Discharged at last, the next chapter could truly begin.

John held Martha's hand, walking out to the car. He felt deeply grateful. Through the amazing work of the medical staff, love, and encouragement from family and friends, he overcame the challenge. The home was waiting, and the future looked bright.

***

As Martha helped John up the front steps of their house, Scruffy peered anxiously out the window. The moment he heard the door open, he went wild with joy! "Scruffy, no jumping!" Martha cautioned with a laugh. But the old dog was too overjoyed to contain himself. He zoomed up to John, tail wagging a mile a minute, and planted puppy kisses all over John's face.

John dropped to his knees with a chuckle, wrapping Scruffy in a big hug. "There's my good boy! I missed you too." Scruffy whimpered and whined, nuzzling close, so happy to have John home at last.

Martha watched them with tears in her eyes, warmed by Scruffy's pure, unconditional love. "See how loved you are, John? We've all been waiting so patiently for this day."

Later, as John relaxed on the couch, Scruffy curled up cheerfully at his feet, keeping a watchful eye on his returned human. A reminder of the little blessings home provided and the joy of being in each other's company once more.

Martha worked hard in the kitchen all afternoon, determined to pamper John with small comforts after his long absence. She knew roast chicken was at the top of his list, so an herb-rubbed bird baked to golden perfection took center stage.

But Martha didn't forget John's side loves either. Creamed corn, flaky biscuits, and mashed potatoes swirling with gravy begged to be enjoyed. Dessert awaited, too: a sliced apple tart, lightly sweetened according to the diet.

Now, as they sat down together, John's face showed his appreciation. "You sure know how to welcome a man home, darling. I had almost forgotten what real food tasted like in that place."

Martha beamed, so happy to nourish both his body and soul once more within their walls. It seemed like old habits die hard for John! As his loving wife, Martha knew she'd have to keep a watchful eye on his salt intake.

While the meal was delicious, she noticed John adding a few extra shakes of salt here and there when he thought she wasn't looking. With a gentle, motherly smile, Martha laid her hand over his.

"I know it's hard to break from what you're used to, honey. But we must find new ways for your taste buds to enjoy food without harming your heart. Might I interest you in some fresh cracked pepper or dried herbs to liven things up?"

John grumbled a bit but agreed. He couldn't deny this woman anything, especially after all her care. From now on, Martha decided they'd explore new low-sodium seasonings together, turning meal prep into bonding time.

With patience and creativity, even an admitted foodie like John might come to appreciate healthier options nearly as much as his old standards. One step at a time, Martha walked beside him on this journey, focused on the destination: many more years of making joyful memories at home.

While John delighted in being home, old habits proved hard to break. His medications sat untouched some days when he felt alright. He continued to be non-compliant with his dietary recommendations. Once Martha cooked a low-salt vegetable meal, John pushed the veggies around his plate glumly. "I just don't see how I can give up that yummy food for good. It's not fair!"

As for exercises, John knew turning his routine around wouldn't be simple either.

Martha thought that it would be an uphill battle to get him to fully comply. "I know you're not fond of this diet, honey, but for your heart, we must be cautious. Would you really choose food over our future years together? Your health is the most precious gift," she said softly.

But gazing at Martha's kind, worn face, John steeled his resolve. Nothing mattered more than her and the life they had left to share. Hopefully, he would find a way to transform.

***

The next morning, they sat for an hour over coffee, catching up on this and that. "Things are finally looking up," John said with a smile. Martha nodded warmly. "Say thanks to our friends who kept you going," John continued. "All those visits, flowers, and prayers... I don't know where I would be without them."

Martha sipped coffee and said, "They regularly checked about your health and prayed for your recovery, darling. But it is time we repay their kindness somehow." She paused, thinking. "Say, what do you think about throwing a get-together for everyone?" John lit up.

"What a good idea, Martha! It would be the nicest way to share our gratitude. Bet they'd all love that." He beamed.

"Then it's settled," Martha declared. "A party to celebrate your recovery and the community's care. I'll start making calls."

And so, the plans were set in motion, with excitement growing each day. John and Martha busied themselves, preparing for the big day. Twinkling lights and pine boughs transformed their home into a winter wonderland.

A mouthwatering feast took shape in the kitchen. Roast turkey, dressing, potatoes, and all the fixings. Martha's mincemeat pie and John's favorite eggnog provided festive finishing touches.

When the doorbell rang and guests streamed in, warm greetings and hugs filled the air. "So good to see you up and about!" said neighbors Nancy and Bill. Friend Justin chuckled, "Don't worry, I came empty-handed—doctor's orders!"

They gathered around the tree, taking turns reading funny Christmas crackers. Laughter rang out as presents were unwrapped and songs were sung. As the evening wound down, John gave thanks to all the friends who had rallied around them through difficult days. "Your friendship and prayers have meant the world to Martha and me. From the bottom of our hearts, Merry Christmas, and God bless you all!"

As the party continued in full swing, the conversation naturally turned to topics close to their agricultural community. Justin chuckled about the debates over crop prices versus production costs. "If these fertilizer prices don't come down, I may have to plant fallow fields next season!"

Nancy nodded knowingly. "And don't even get me started on land values. How are folks our age supposed to retire someday?" Bill shook his head. "My wife and I barely made it to the next town clinic last month; the roads were so bad after the freeze. It ain't right for rural folks."

John listened intently, grateful to be back among friends and family. "Times are changing faster than these old bones!" he quipped. More seriously, he said, "We all must look out for our well-being as best we can. No use tending fields if we're not around to see the harvest!"

The friends all laughed and agreed, raising their drinks in a toast. "To your health, John, and many more years keeping us all in line!" Cheers and happiness echoed through the cozy home well into the night.

As the conversation turned to healthcare, Bill shared with John, "You know, I think I've found a good primary care doctor for people like us. He just set up a practice about an hour's drive from where we live. He's a real expert and seems to actually listen."

John nodded thoughtfully. Maintaining his health was paramount now. "Maybe I'll call his office and see if he's taking new patients. Getting in with someone who is prevention-minded sounds wise."

Martha squeezed his arm, smiling. "I think that's a wonderful idea, dear. A doctor we can rely on will put my mind at ease."

Perhaps this new physician could help John stay on track to reap many more harvests with his cherished friends and family. One step at a time, together they navigated the changes of aging, keeping spirits bright as colorful leaves fell on their bountiful land.

As Justin recounted getting his colonoscopy just in time, Nancy smiled and said, "Amen to that, brother. My yearly mammogram caught something tiny, and now, who's to say I won't make it to 100?"

Bill, ever the optimist, raised his glass. "And here's to modern medicine! Didn't that COVID shot save my hide, despite my sugar and high blood pressure?"

Martha turned thoughtfully. "There are lessons here that our age can't afford to forget. Maybe part of getting healthy is learning from each other, too. What tests should be asked for, and should vaccines not be overlooked? How's that for a New Year's resolution we old timers can toast to?"

Glasses raised with a cheer; the friends smirked at their 'officially senior' title but took the message to heart. Together, through open talks about trials and joys, their community stayed strong.

As the last guests headed home under a blanket of stars, John and Martha smiled. This Christmas was the merriest one yet, in their loving home together once more.

John sat down with Martha the day after Christmas for a heartfelt discussion. The holiday lifted his spirits but also reminded him of his health and family commitments.

"You've stood by me through this whole suffering, darling," John said, taking her hand. "And seeing our friends and community, I know how blessed we are. From here on, I want to do right by you—eat smarter, take medicines regularly, and exercise more regularly."

Martha's eyes watered at his resolve. "All I've ever wanted is for us to grow old together, happy and healthy." If focusing on wellness will give us that, then I'm right by your side as always, dear."

John also decided to touch base with Henry, who had missed the party for good reason, tending to his daughter Sam and wife Lisa. After ringing Henry, he smiled to hear of snow, cookies, and Christmas fun at the house. "Family comes first, always will. Just keeping you in our thoughts and prayers with each new day's sun."

With a commitment to health and kin all around, John started the New Year grateful for life's greatest gifts. Love of community, love of home, and love that sees one through every season.

***

It was just after the New Year had begun when the phone started ringing off the hook at Martha and John's place. "Another call already?" John chuckled as Martha picked up the phone. But her eyes went wide. "For you, darling. Sounds important."

John took the phone curiously. "Hello?" He gasped. "Michael, is that you?"

On the other end, Michael began speaking gently. "How's your health doing? Happy New Year, Dad. I, uh... I just wanted to call and wish you the best. I heard about your health scare. Henry has been leaving voicemails on my phone."

John was overcome. "I... I appreciate that, son. Really, I do. Love and support from family and friends lifted my spirits and helped me recover. I hoped and prayed that you and your family could come and visit in time."

Then little voices piped up, "Grandpa!" John broke down in tears. Michael's wife, Ashley, talked with John about his health. From then on, the calls kept coming, family catching up and sharing hopes for this fresh year. But Michael's surprise was to trump all the others.

As the phone call progressed, Michael opened up to John about past regrets. "Dad, I was ashamed after leaving like that," Michael said hesitantly. "I thought you would be disappointed in me for not making it in the city."

John shook his head gently. "Son, I only ever wanted your happiness."

Michael sighed. "I know... but it was hard going at first. Long hours, tiny place, missing home something fierce." His voice grew thick. "It took all the courage inside me just to get through each day in the big city."

Nodding, John listened without judgment as Michael recounted his struggles. But then his tone lifted slightly. "A few years ago, I finally caught a break. I saved up and opened my own music and dance studio!" Pride shone through. "Now I'm teaching what I love with roots put down at last."

Michael breathed deeply, relief mixing with joy. "Which is why, after so long, I needed you to hear it from me. Our past is past; I just want to support you however I can, Dad, even from afar. If you'll have me..."

"Oh, Michael, of course!" John replied fondly. The bonds of the family ran deeper than any distance.

Going off to the big city for work must've filled the days in a rush at first. But it sounded like I was learning life's deeper lessons—that cherished people were what mattered most when everything was said and done.

Being apart helped me appreciate home bonds in a new light. Distance sometimes has a way of clarifying perspectives. Michael said my dreams took me far away, but I always had you all tucked deep in my soul.

John smiled warmly. "That's wonderful to hear, son. I always knew you would find your way. You keep shining like you do. And know that this will always be your harbor in any storm. A body could fly high, but you always have solid roots to return to."

As John said his goodbyes, bleary-eyed but beaming, Martha embraced him tightly. "What a blessed day, John. Old wounds healed, and joy was rekindled. Isn't renewal just grand?" John just nodded, grinning through his tears. His heart had never felt fuller.

John rang Henry and excitedly told him about Michael's surprise phone call. "Can you believe it, Henry?" John said it gleefully. "My boy Michael finally got in touch after all these years!"

Henry was silent for a moment. "Hmm. It took him long enough to return my voicemails, I'll say. But go on, what did he have to say for himself?" John recounted Michael's tale of struggle and success, then continued. "He wants to repair things with the family and be here for us however he's able."

At this, Henry's expression softened. "Well, I can't fault the lad for chasing his heart and dreams. I am happy that he is settled in his life now. I hope Michael and Cara's families also start getting along soon." He sighed, his shoulders relaxing. "Water under the bridge now, I suppose."

John smiled, relief smoothing his weary features. "It means the world to have you both in my corner once more. Maybe now, with time, those old bridges can be rebuilt." Hope shone on the horizon, whereas before, there was only distance and regret. And that, Henry knew, was thanks enough.

"Well, hello there, my girl Swifty!" John chuckled as Sam excitedly said hello to him. Lisa also offered New Year's wishes and asked John to take care of his health. But ever the optimist, John reassured them all. "This old coot's not going anywhere just yet! I'm just going to take care of myself properly from here on out."

"Swifty, what are your resolutions this year?" he asked. "Well, big grandpa, I want to learn guitar!" Sam said it excitedly. "Been borrowing Dad's but think it's time I got my own."

John smiled. "A fine goal, that is. Anything else?" Sam frowned thoughtfully. "Mom's always saying I'm glued to my phone. The reels are so addictive. They keep coming one after the other, according to my interests, and before I know it, I've spent so much time watching them. I am also spending a lot of time on social media. So, I'm going to cut back screen time and read more books instead."

"Wise girl," John nodded approvingly. Just then, another call rang; it was Cara calling. After greetings and well wishes, Cara talked about adjusting priorities accordingly. I am trying to balance my personal and professional life. I want to take care of myself. Our loved ones were here for a blink, then gone all too soon. Cara realized that, so she was cutting the fluff to attend to what really filled her soul.

John asked his grandson Daniel if he had any plans for self-improvement this year. As a matter of fact, Daniel replied, "I aim to improve my tennis serve. I've been practicing my swing, but I need to add some more energy and spin to my serve. I want to win more tennis tournaments this year."

"An athletic resolution; I can't argue with that!" John chuckled. With such promise and dedication around him, he had a fine feeling this would be their best year yet.

As they said their goodbyes, promising to visit come Thanksgiving time, John sat holding the memory of their call close. Beside him, Martha smiled knowingly at his New

Year's resolution - perhaps a small step but one of commitment stemming from lessons hard learned.

**

John and Henry were enjoying a quiet morning together at John's home. Henry was thinking about his father's health. "Dad, I think it's time we schedule an appointment with the doctor," Henry said gently.

John waved him off. "Now, son, I've never felt better. This old body's still got some miles left in it." But Henry insisted. "Humor me, dad. It'll put this worried mind of mine at ease." He picked up the phone and dialed the clinic John's friend Bill suggested at the party. The receptionist answered cheerily. "Hello there, what can I do for you?"

"It's about my dad," Henry explained. "I thought it was best he comes in for a check-up; make sure everything's running smoothly." The receptionist said kindly, "Let me see... I can squeeze him in on Thursday at 2 o'clock. Okay?"

"Thursday's perfect, thank you," Henry replied. He hung up and smiled at his stubborn father. "Don't fuss now. The appointment's made. A body's health is nothing to neglect, so I'll take you whether you like it or not." John laughed. "Alright, son, I know when I'm beaten. We'll go see the doctor."

When John arrived for his appointment, the nurse greeted him warmly. The nurse took John's vitals and checked his height. "Alright, sir, if you'll step on the scale... it looks like you're up a few pounds, and your blood pressure is elevated," the nurse noted.

"John, your body mass index, or BMI is high. It puts you in the obesity range based on your height and weight. BMI isn't perfect, but it is good for initial screening. It's a simple, low-cost metric for identifying if a patient is underweight, overweight, or has obesity."

John hmmed at this new information. "I know I have been putting on extra pounds in the last few years since I cut back on my work. But I never heard anyone before telling me that I have obesity." He wondered to himself if that might be why Sam calls him "Big Grandpa."

The nurse asked screening questions for depression and suicide risk. She also inquired about alcohol, smoking, and illegal drug use. "Alright, let me inform the physician that you are ready," the nurse said.

The physician entered the room and introduced himself. John and Henry expressed appreciation for the doctor setting up his practice in the rural community. Upon learning of the lack of primary care access in the area for some time, the doctor acknowledged this challenge. "I'm aware many rural communities struggle with healthcare deserts," the doctor noted. Primary care services would significantly improve health outcomes, increase life span, and lower costs across our healthcare system, the doctor said, his voice filled with conviction.

As the examination began, the physician expressed his commitment to serving patients from all parts of the region. "Some must drive quite a long way, which is certainly not ideal," he remarked.

After going over the vital signs and health records from John's hospital stay, he performed a detailed history and physical examination of John. John, "You are a lucky man. You survived a major health scare."

I see you have diabetes and hypertension. Your blood pressure is high, the doctor said, his eyes locking onto John's. You are on good medicines, but your blood pressure is running high. Are you taking your medicines regularly?

John admitted that he has been neglecting to take his medicines. Medication compliance, regular follow-ups with physicians, and lifestyle changes like a healthy diet and exercise are very important for maintaining your health.

"Millions with diabetes, hypertension, or other chronic medical conditions can significantly lower the complications from these diseases and medical costs with proper primary care management."

"Did you ever get a colonoscopy done?" asked the doctor. John replied, "No, doctor."

"Let me refer you to a gastroenterologist for screening colonoscopy. I will also order a few more blood tests. You are also due for vaccines like the flu and pneumonia," said the doctor.

Prevention is better than cure. As your primary care doctor, preventing health issues will be my primary focus. I think it's important you understand how our primary care model supports that goal. At its core, primary care provides continuity of medical care; we aim to be your trusted partner over the long run and improve your quality of life.

Furthermore, annual exams and health screenings allow us to catch minor health issues early before they get worse. Even asymptomatic check-ups can uncover risk factors or signs of developing diseases. Early detection of health conditions like breast, cervical, or colorectal cancer can lead to better treatment outcomes and improved survival rates.

I'll also make sure you have the knowledge and resources needed to take an active role in your own healthcare. Things like understanding a new medication or lifestyle changes empower you at home. "Health literacy has real impacts."

Henry nodded, clearly absorbing the information. He brought up the topic of John's non-adherence to diet changes. The nurse also informed us that John has obesity.

The physician turned to John and asked him to talk more about his diet and weight changes. The physician listened with empathy regarding John's challenges with diet compliance and recent weight gain. John wanted to hear more from the physician regarding obesity.

The physician praised John for his willingness to learn more about obesity. "Okay, as your doctor, let me tell you the true health implications obesity presents."

"Obesity is a chronic, complex, and recurrent disease. It is increasing in numbers right in front of our eyes. One in four Americans might have severe obesity by 2030. Unfortunately, obesity in children is also on the rise."

Henry leaned forward, clearly concerned.

"Our food portion sizes increased while physical activity had declined. And it wasn't simply an issue of appearance;

every organ system can be affected because of obesity. Patients with obesity are at risk of developing medical conditions like heart attack, stroke, sleep apnea, hypertension and diabetes. Not just these conditions, there is also an increased risk of cancer, liver injury, and depression. Even modest weight loss is beneficial."

With our busy schedules, we do not take time to cook fresh food and instead depend on ultra-processed food. This ultra-processed food, which has different additives added to it, also plays a big role in increasing obesity.

The doctor paused, letting his words resonate. "Certain medical conditions like hypothyroidism or Cushing's syndrome could contribute to weight gain in some cases. Genetics, stress, sleep deprivation, and obesity-inducing medicines also played a role for some individuals."

John nodded, listening intently.

"I wanted to paint a full picture of what we're up against with this condition, John," the doctor said. "But working together, lifestyle changes were definitely possible. Small steps like mindful eating and regular exercise could yield great results over the long run."

"It's reassuring how far research has come in understanding obesity's underlying biological mechanisms," the doctor continued. "This knowledge is helpful to advance new pharmacological therapies. Some medications showed real promise at promoting significant weight loss along with other health benefits."

Henry nodded, clearly absorbing the information.

"Surgery and endoscopic procedures remained a viable option for those who qualify for the procedure," the doctor said. "Insurance coverage had certainly helped greater numbers of appropriate patients access this surgery path."

John's eyes widened slightly, considering the possibilities.

"However, as we discussed, any weight loss intervention still required lasting lifestyle modifications for success," the doctor emphasized.

Crash diets or drastic calorie cutting were rarely effective long-term solutions. Metabolism and appetite will adjust after weight loss, so maintenance takes a serious commitment to healthier behaviors.

"Eating a healthy and balanced meal plate that contains proteins like lean meat, fish, legumes, whole grains, vegetables, fruits, and healthy fats like nuts, avocado, and dairy is ideal."

"Make a habit to read food labels when you pick food items at the grocery store. It can empower you to make more informed choices," the doctor continued.

Henry smiled, liking the practical advice.

While certain exercises may not appeal, the simple act of moving more each day is truly valuable. And around 150 minutes per week of activities like walking, light strength exercises, or simple resistance exercises can definitely aid your goals."

The doctor said warmly, "John, my role is to support your well-being journey. Why don't we schedule some additional visits to check in on non-scale victories, troubleshoot challenges, and ensure you have all the education and encouragement you need?"

John and Henry exchanged a glance, both feeling more hopeful.

Remember, too, that health comes in many forms. Mental health is just as vital, so be kind to yourself in this process.

"Does this help explain my philosophy of care, John?" He asked and said, "I want you to feel supported as your health advocate. Both your physical health and mental well-being are important to address holistically."

John nodded thoughtfully, absorbing the doctor's words. He felt a renewed sense of commitment to his own health journey.

"When individuals take care of their health proactively, the ability to contribute financially and remain productive members of the workforce becomes much more attainable," the doctor said, his tone optimistic. "When the population is healthier, the economy will also be stronger."

Henry looked at his dad, sensing his father's renewed resolve. John returned the gesture, feeling more hopeful than he had in a long time.

"Thank you, doctor, for the valuable information and your commitment to serve us. Our communities deserve access to full primary care services that broadly address physical, mental, and social well-being," Henry said, his voice steady.

"The shortage of primary care physicians in the near future is truly alarming," the doctor said, his tone serious. That large gap risks leaving millions of Americans without a primary care provider.

The doctor continued, "It's unfortunate but true that primary care physicians often face significant burnout from all the paperwork they have to deal with."

Interventions like increasing training slots and loan forgiveness for those committing to primary care practice would incentivize new providers. Reimbursement rates also require adjustments. Standardizing documentation and streamlining billing could save time for more patient-facing work.

"With collaborative reforms between medical societies and policymakers, I hope to see the primary care field retain its appeal and sustainability for future generations of healers," the doctor said, with earnestness in his eyes.

"The well-being of communities demands no less. This is an ongoing challenge, but progress takes open and empathetic discussions like ours," said the doctor.

John nodded, his attention fully on the doctor, absorbing every word. Henry, sitting beside him, leaned in closer, clearly invested in the conversation.

Nurse practitioners and physician assistants supervised by physicians could help offset physician shortages in underserved areas. With proper training and oversight, they are invaluable partners in providing medical care to these areas.

The doctor paused, letting the gravity of the situation sink in. John felt a knot form in his stomach, the weight of the information-heavy on his mind.

"Our patients deserve no less than to have their basic healthcare needs met by skilled clinicians in their own communities. This is the kind of 'big picture' discussion I find most rewarding in this field," the doctor said with a slight smile, trying to lighten the mood.

"Telehealth expands our reach, as seen clearly during the pandemic," the doctor continued, his expression serious yet hopeful. "With adequate reimbursement, it can help close gaps in underserved communities. Technology hopefully bridges distance barriers between patients and their care teams."

With collective effort and continued reforms, I know we can strengthen this critical foundation of the healthcare system nationwide and advance the health of all.

The doctor gently concluded the conversation, "But let's focus on small, manageable shifts you feel good about starting. I will ask my receptionist to make a follow-up appointment in a month. My door is always open if you need help and guidance. Take care of your health, John."

Chapter 6

John exhaled as he settled onto the couch, already winded from the short walk home. It had been a few days since he saw his primary care physician. Initially, he was motivated and made efforts to adhere to the doctor's instructions. Very soon, he reverted to his old habits.

Martha watched sadly as John added extra salt without thinking. She knew how much he enjoyed socializing but was worried as he went out to a nearby restaurant more often while skipping his medications.

Within days, John's legs and stomach had noticeably swollen. His weight increased by several pounds in a week. He kept his head end of the bed elevated while sleeping with pillows to help with shortness of breath. He had to get up in the middle of the night to open the window to catch air. Even light chores left him panting. One night, a worrying crackling sound woke Martha as John struggled to breathe.

Martha watched John worry, his breathing growing shallower. John got into his recliner and finally fell asleep. The next morning, Martha called the primary care doctor's clinic. The doctor suggested that John take an extra dose of his water pill and go to the nearby emergency room for further work up.

The blizzard outside was wild, with snow falling heavily from the sky. The wind was howling, making the trees sway back and forth. Everything was covered in a thick, white blanket of snow. The driveway was buried under a deep pile of snow.

Martha knew she had to get John to the hospital, but the blizzard made it very hard. She bundled up in warm clothes, put on the gloves and stepped outside, feeling the cold wind hit her face.

The snow was so deep that every step was difficult. She had trouble starting the snow blower. The snow blower is a big machine that can move a lot of snow quickly. She then grabbed a shovel and started to clear the snow, but it was heavy and hard to move. Her arms hurt, and she was out of breath, but she kept going because she knew John needed help.

Across the street, their neighbor Justin saw Martha struggling. He knew she needed help, so he put on his coat and gloves and came over with his snow blower.

"Martha, let me help you," Justin said, his voice kind.

Martha looked up and felt relieved to see her neighbor. "Thank you, Justin," she said. She was glad he was there to help.

Together, they cleared the driveway much faster. The snow blower made the job easier, and soon, the path was clear. While they worked, Martha told Justin how sick John was. She was very worried about him because he was having trouble breathing.

Justin listened and knew they needed to get John to the hospital, but the roads were very dangerous because of the snow. "Martha, it's too risky for you to drive. Let me take you and John to the hospital in my truck. It's safer that way," Justin said.

Martha thought about it for a moment. She didn't want to ask for help, but she knew Justin was right. The roads were too bad for her to drive alone. "Okay, Justin. Thank you," she said.

Justin smiled. "That's what neighbors are for," he said. They went back inside, where John was waiting. They wrapped him in warm blankets and helped him into the back seat of Justin's truck. The truck was warm inside, which felt nice compared to the cold outside. Justin started driving slowly through the snow, carefully making his way to the hospital.

The roads were very slippery, and it was hard to see because the snow was falling so fast. But Justin was careful, and they made their way through the blizzard, making sure John got the help he needed.

In the truck, John cracked jokes and teased Justin despite his labored breaths. Laughter helped lighten their heavy hearts. Justin recounted more of John's kindness, the harvest help, and more.

Being kind to others and helping each other can help overcome challenges, creating a positive environment and strong communities.

At last, they arrived at the nearby emergency room, rushing John inside out of the biting winds. Though the storm raged outwardly, companionship and care warmed from within, thanks to the kindheartedness of neighbors in a town where every act of support could mean the difference between struggle and survival.

John was taken into the emergency room for examination. While waiting in the emergency room, Martha got a call from Lisa. Lisa called to check on how they were doing. Henry was out of town for office work. Martha described

John's struggles with his breathlessness and their trip to the emergency room. Lisa got worried and rushed to the emergency room in blizzard conditions to support them. Sam stayed at home.

In the emergency room, Lisa hugged Martha. She felt grateful and thanked Justin for helping them in need. "How's dad doing?" Martha said, "Not good. The doctors are examining him."

Lisa put a hand on Martha's arm. "You've always been there for me, like when Sam was born, and you watched her so Henry and I could work." Martha and John would babysit Sam whenever necessary, allowing Lisa to teach. They always helped when Lisa and Henry were busy.

Parenting is a rewarding journey, but at times, it can be challenging, like the expensive daycare services. Having family support like Lisa and Henry's from Martha and John can ease some of these challenges. They can also provide emotional support when needed and make the parenting experience more fulfilling.

When Lisa had a stretch of emotional downturn after the death of her mother, Henry and his family supported Lisa through her recovery from the depression phase. Now, John and Martha needed her support. Lisa said she wanted to return the favor and help however she could.

The emergency room physician examined John and recommended he stay in the hospital for close monitoring and further treatment of his congestive heart failure. The doctor also informed me that John is having a rapid, irregular heartbeat called atrial fibrillation.

"His heart rate needs to be controlled as well. We will start medicines to control his heart rate. We will also start him on a blood thinner to prevent strokes. We will give him intravenous medicines to take out more fluid from his body. We will place him on supplemental oxygen and watch his electrolytes and kidney numbers closely," said the emergency room physician.

Martha felt worried as the doctor explained John's condition. She listened carefully, trying to understand every word, but all she could think about was how much John had already been through. The news about his heart having an irregular beat made her heart sink even further. The doctor's calm, clinical words couldn't mask the seriousness of the situation.

As the doctor talked about the treatment plan for keeping John in the hospital, controlling his heart rate, using blood thinners and starting IV medicines, Martha's anxiety grew.

She knew these steps were necessary, but the thought of John enduring more procedures and treatments weighed heavily on her heart. She was deeply worried about the toll this was taking on him, both physically and emotionally.

Martha's eyes filled with tears, and she tried to hold back. She felt a mixture of fear and sadness. Fear of what could happen next and sadness for the man she loved, who was struggling so much.

But beneath it all, there was a quiet strength. She knew she had to be strong for John, even when she felt like her own heart might break. She squeezed his hand gently, her way of letting him know she was there for him, no matter what.

The next day, Henry returned from the office trip. He rushed directly to John's hospital room, anxious to see his father after the worrying news. "How are you feeling, Dad?"

John smiled weakly. "Good to see you, son. Not too bad, all things considered." Just then, a hospital representative entered. "John, I have some forms regarding your Medicare status."

As she explained John's observation level of care, confusion crossed both Henry's and John's faces. "I don't understand. We thought dad was admitted to the hospital," Henry asked.

The representative nodded. "That's a common misunderstanding. Let me explain the difference between inpatient level of care and observation level of care."

She then outlined the key points clearly for them: "Inpatient level of care requires at least two midnights of hospital stay for medical necessity with few exceptions versus observation level of care being a shorter outpatient stay with close monitoring to determine if a patient needs an inpatient hospital admission or can be discharged from the hospital.

The level of care status can influence the expenses for diagnostic tests and treatments provided in the hospital. Additionally, if you need to be discharged from the hospital to a nursing home, your level of care status can impact the coverage for nursing home expenses.

The representative went on to explain that the observation level of care is covered under Medicare Part B versus the inpatient level of care under Medicare Part A. If a patient only has Medicare Part A, then the patient may be responsible for the hospital bill for the observation level of care. Also, if a Medicare patient has to go to a nursing home after discharge from the hospital, they must have at least 3 inpatient level of care overnight stays in the hospital and skilled care needs for the nursing home stay to be covered by Medicare. Skilled care needs include services like physical therapy and occupational therapy.

Henry listened attentively, slowly comprehending the nuance. "I see. So, dad is considered to have an observation level of care status since the doctor thinks he'll require less than two-midnight stay in the hospital to treat his illness?"

"Precisely," the representative replied. But there are a few exceptions to this two-midnight rule.

John sighed. "It's a lot to take in, but I'm glad you took the time to walk us through it thoroughly."

The next day brought an update: a physician advisor from utilization management carefully reviewed John's chart and determined an inpatient level of care is now warranted, expecting a minimum two-midnight stay to treat John's medical condition.

"The hospitalist upgraded Dad's status then?" asked Henry. "Yes, based on his medical necessity to stay longer in the hospital to treat his congestive heart failure and atrial fibrillation," she replied.

Henry breathed a sigh of relief upon hearing John was receiving the correct level of care. While John's health was most important now, the representative was heartened by this difficult period, which also highlighted the hospital's thoughtful culture of support.

John had an ultrasound of his heart. His pumping of the heart reduced even further to 20 percent. The hospitalist and the cardiologist worked as a team to further adjust his medicines. His symptoms gradually improved during the hospitalization.

Henry requested his boss again for time off to take care of his dad; it was approved without hesitation. "It is reassuring to hear that your dad is steadily improving," said Henry's boss. He had a background in the healthcare insurance industry before he transitioned to establishing his own mortgage firm. He was highly regarded by his staff for his supportive nature.

He wanted his staff to have a work-life balance and provided them with a flexible work schedule and ample paid time off. He believed that a positive and productive work environment is created when an employer supports the well-being of employees.

For the next three days, Henry and Martha stayed with John in the hospital. His clinical status improved, and he was off supplemental oxygen. His intravenous medicines were transitioned to oral medicines. He was discharged from the hospital on increased doses of water pills, heart rate control medicines, and blood thinner.

***

Henry returned to work, but his personal challenges were spilling into the work environment and interfering with his work performance. Henry seemed distracted at work, and his boss took notice of this.

He wanted to have a friendly dialogue with Henry, provide moral support, and see how he could help more. "Why don't we grab lunch today, my treat?" Henry's boss suggested.

"Sure, I will bring my car to the front entrance. We can head to the restaurant together," said Henry.

Over burgers at the diner, Henry's boss asked, "Is everything alright? You seem weighed down."

Henry sighed. "It's my dad. His health is declining, and it's a lot to manage on top of everything else."

His boss listened supportively. "I can't imagine the stress you're under. Is there any way the company can help relieve some pressure?"

Hoping to lighten his mood, he asked, "Didn't Lisa recommend you to us years ago after your honorable military discharge? How is she doing? Lisa's dad and I shared a strong friendship while he was alive, and I've known Lisa since she was a child."

She is fine, Henry replied. "Yes, she knew I was struggling to find work and put in a good word." To create a pleasant atmosphere, Henry's boss asked, "How did Lisa and your paths cross?"

A smile appeared on Henry's face. He went on to explain, "After completing contracted obligations with the military, I decided to come back and stay close to my parents. I knew they would need my help as they got older. My other siblings went far away to the East and West coasts."

Henry began, recalling the events that led him to Lisa. "It was the 2007-2008 financial crisis at that time. Jobs were hard to find, and nothing was certain. Along with actively pursuing career opportunities, I was helping my dad with farming at the time.

One day, while listening to the radio, I heard a call for volunteers at the local elementary school's upcoming "Fun Run" event. With spare time on my hands and job searching during the recession, I decided to help out.

When I arrived at the school, the principal immediately put me to work setting up for the "Fun Run" event.

I thoroughly enjoyed and put forth my best effort at the "Fun Run" celebration. I cheerfully encouraged kids along the course and lifted the spirits of the children and the school staff.

Though humble work, finding purpose in service to the community filled an important need. In large and small acts of kindness, humanity weathers even the bleakest of times.

Impressed by my strong work ethic and cheerful manner, the principal began offering odd jobs around the school as needs arose. The principal would have loved to offer me a permanent job at the school, but they could not create any new openings, given the financial turmoil from the recession. I still enjoyed staying busy and seeing the children's smiling faces.

As I worked more shifts at the school, I began observing Lisa, a third-grade teacher who always kept to herself. She seemed withdrawn from her colleagues.

Concerned, I gently asked other staff members what they knew. I learned of Lisa's hardships—her mother's death, and a recent breakup, leaving her grief-stricken. No wonder she appeared depressed, bearing such personal struggles by herself.

My heart ached for her. Though strangers, I wanted to offer a compassionate ear. Starting small, I began greeting Lisa warmly each day, hoping smiles and polite questions might chip away at her isolation.

At first, she barely responded, her eyes downcast, and she lacked facial expression. I did not give up, and I knew I could assist her in overcoming her struggles with patience and good humor. I recalled a discussion with one of her colleagues where cooking came up as Lisa's passion.

During one of the encounters with Lisa, I asked, "Lisa, what's your favorite thing to cook? Maybe sharing a recipe could brighten both our days." A glimmer of interest sparked in her eyes, and to my delight, she began answering in full sentences.

A connection was forming, however fragile. In small ways like this, caring souls can lend a helping hand and strengthen one another.

Knowing her cooking talents, I suggested Lisa join the cooking club in a nearby town. There, she slowly began connecting with others through a cherished hobby. Her spirit lifted in kind ways, much like how preparing food nourishes bodies.

Lisa started opening up more about her mental challenges with me. She was going through persistent and prolonged emotional pain from the unexpected loss of her mother. She already lost her father while she was in high school. She was having intense thoughts about her mother. She was going through complicated grief. Her struggles were compounded by a breakup with her boyfriend. She went into depression, became socially withdrawn, and stopped enjoying the things she used to like before.

Listening to Lisa, I was more committed to further assisting her well-being beyond classroom walls. I invited her on walks and exercises, nurturing mental and physical health alike. I also asked her to join me for swimming sessions. Gradually, the distance between us closed through nothing but care, empathy, and time.

A "Battle of the Books" competition is approaching at the school, and I offered to train Lisa's students for it. Together, Lisa and I worked with her class to prepare the students for the competition. Ultimately, Lisa's class emerged victorious. This brought great happiness to Lisa, who hadn't experienced such success in a long time due to her personal challenges. This victory brought her much-needed joy.

One day, I introduced Lisa to my parents, and they immediately hit it off. This connection helped ease some of Lisa's suffering from losing her mother, as she found a motherly figure in Martha.

I even offered Lisa the opportunity to meet a mental health specialist. She initially refused but later agreed. This visit helped Lisa with coping strategies, relaxation techniques, and positive thinking and provided her with mental health literacy to overcome the stigma associated with mental health. Lisa finally emerged from her difficult period and was back to her usual self.

In my search for a stable job, life felt like an endless series of closed doors. Each application and each interview seemed to lead nowhere, leaving me in a place of uncertainty and frustration. My position at the school was temporary, and as much as I cherished it, I knew it couldn't last forever. The anxiety of not finding permanent work weighed heavily on me, and I confided in Lisa about these struggles.

Lisa, despite her own battles with mental health, listened with compassion. She understood the fears that come with uncertainty and the desire for something stable. Recognizing my need for a break, she referred me to you, hoping that this opportunity might be the one to finally anchor me in place.

When we met, and you offered me a permanent position at your company, it felt like a lifeline thrown to a man adrift at sea. It wasn't just a job; it was the stability I had been searching for, the foundation on which I could start building again.

Lisa's journey, too, was one of transformation. After navigating her struggles, she emerged with a renewed sense of purpose, driven to make a difference in the community.

She saw clearly how mental health was not just an individual battle but a collective one, affecting every part of our lives, from relationships to work to overall well-being. At the local Parent Teacher Association (PTA) meeting, her passion shone through as she spoke. She was no longer just a survivor of her struggles but a warrior for change.

"Start small," she urged the anxious mother. "Small changes can have big impacts. Let's create a culture where mental health is spoken about openly, where our children feel safe to express themselves, and where stigma has no place."

The principal, moved by her words, suggested that Lisa and I co-lead a wellness workshop for parents. It was a chance to take what we had both learned and use it to help others. In that moment, I realized how far we had both come—two people who had been struggling in the dark, now standing in the light, ready to guide others towards it.

In every workshop, Lisa's voice rang clear, speaking on the connections between mental health and every facet of life. She talked about how untreated mental health issues could ripple through a person's life, affecting not just their physical health but their relationships, their work, and their very sense of self. She spoke with the authority of someone who had lived through the darkness and found her way back to the light.

"It is OK to talk with others about your mental health struggles and get help if needed. I talked with Henry about my struggles, and it helped me a lot," said Lisa.

Listening to her, I felt a deep sense of pride and gratitude. Together, we had taken our individual struggles and turned them into something meaningful, something that could help others. It wasn't just about overcoming challenges anymore; it was about using those challenges to build something better for us and for our community."

Henry's boss, hearing his story, saw it for what it was. A testament to the power of support, understanding, and resilience.

"It's truly remarkable," he said, "how the two of you, through your struggles, have not only found strength in each other but have also become a source of inspiration for others. In a world full of storms, you both found a way to shelter each other and, in doing so, illuminated the path forward."

And he was right. Their bond had grown in ways neither of us could have predicted. What began as two individuals grappling with their own challenges had evolved into a partnership grounded in empathy, respect, and a shared mission to make things better.

The arrival of little Sam completed the picture, representing a symbol of hope and new beginnings. As a family, they found joy in nurturing this new life, in watching Sam grow, and in the knowledge that they had weathered the storm together.

"How about we order some desserts as well? I heard raspberry sorbet is yummy here," said Henry's boss. "Sure, I could go for some dessert, too," said Henry.

While waiting for the desserts, their conversation shifted to discussing the complexities of the healthcare insurance landscape. "Navigating the intricacies of health insurance is like navigating a complex maze. I tried reading about it but got confused. I remember you mentioned having some experience with healthcare insurance. Could you shed some light on this and help me understand the details of health insurance?" said Henry.

"It's so complicated that explaining it could take a fortnight. However, let me give a brief overview," said Henry's boss.

Health care costs can be covered in a few different ways. Some people get help from the government through programs like Medicare, Medicaid, and VA (Veteran Affairs) health insurance. Others have insurance from their employment, or they buy their own health insurance. Unfortunately, some people don't have any health insurance at all.

Medicare is a government program that helps certain groups of people, like those who are 65 years or older, people on dialysis, and those with certain disabilities.

Medicare has four parts: Part A helps pay for services like inpatient hospital stays, nursing home care, and hospice care. Part B helps cover services like outpatient and observation care, doctor visits, mental health care, ambulance rides, and clinical research.

Part C, also known as Medicare Advantage, is run by private companies approved by Medicare. These companies cover everything in Parts A and B and sometimes offer extra benefits like vision and dental care. Part D helps pay for prescription medications.

Medicaid is a program run by both the federal and state governments to help people with limited income and resources. The rules for Medicaid can vary depending on the state you live in. VA health insurance provides care for eligible veterans.

Employer-sponsored insurance is another option, where your job pays for part of your health insurance, and you pay the rest. How much you pay, which doctors you can see, and which hospitals you can visit all depend on the plan your employer offers.

Some people buy their own health insurance, but this can be very expensive. Sadly, there are also millions of people who don't have health insurance at all. They have to pay for all their medical expenses themselves, which can be very difficult.

Henry was trying hard to understand all of this, but it was still confusing. Just then, the waiter brought the bill. Henry's boss, who had been explaining everything, decided to use a comparison to make it easier to understand.

He said, "Think of health insurance like getting passes to a theme park."

"The government gives out season passes to some people, which let them enjoy basic rides. This is like Medicare Part A. If you want to go on more exciting rides, you might have to pay extra, which is like Medicare Part B. If you want snacks and drinks in the park, you have to buy them there, similar to how Medicare Part D covers medications. Sometimes, the government lets private companies sell these passes, too. These companies must follow certain rules, but they can offer different types of passes with various options for what rides you can go on and which theme parks you can visit. This is like Medicare Part C.

For those who work, their employers might buy them season passes. The employer pays for part of the pass, and the employee pays the rest, just like employer-sponsored health insurance.

But some people can't afford any of these passes, so they don't get to go to the theme park. This is like people who don't have health insurance."

Henry found this analogy helpful, but he was sad to learn that so many people don't have access to health care because they don't qualify for government programs, don't have a job that offers health insurance, or can't afford to buy it themselves.

On the way back to the office, Henry's boss also talked about various payment models in health care. For example, with the "fee-for-service" model, doctors and hospitals are paid for each service they provide. The government is trying to create new ways to pay that focus more on the quality and safety of health care provided, like "value-based care." This means doctors and hospitals would get paid based on how well they take care of patients, not just how much care they provide. These new models may help lower costs and improve health care for everyone.

Henry's boss also talked about how important it is to keep coming up with new ideas in health care. Innovation can help make health care cheaper, better, and fairer for everyone. It can also help doctors, nurses, and other medical staff do their jobs better by reducing paperwork and preventing burnout.

At the end of their visit, Henry's boss reassured him, "Your commitment to family and community is admirable. Know that your place at the company is stable regardless of what challenges come up at home." Henry appeared lifted by the listening ear and encouraging words. "Thank you. I really appreciate you taking the time," said Henry.

When Henry arrived home, Lisa greeted him with a warm hug. "How was your day, dear? How was the lunch date with your boss?" Lisa asked jokingly.

"Educational. My boss has a gift for bringing clarity through colorful analogy."

Henry smiled as he reflected on his insightful discussion with his boss. The creative analogies used to explain healthcare concepts were brilliant; things suddenly started making much more sense.

Henry shared an insightful theme park analogy to explain the health insurance landscape. Visualizing it that way helps cut through the complexity. Lisa laughed in recognition of its insights.

"How is Sam doing?" asked Henry.

"She is attending a private online tutorial class, Lisa replied. "I made flax seed crackers and mixed fruit jelly for John and Martha. John had some questions about the blood thinner, so I printed some information about it. Could you deliver it to them?"

"I am planning to visit them this weekend," Henry said. "I will give it to them then.

"By the way, Cara called the home landline phone. She said she was trying to reach you. I updated her about John's health condition," Lisa added.

"Oh, I missed her call! I was at the restaurant with my boss," Henry explained.

The next day, Henry and Lisa went for a walk at the nearby gym. Henry brought up the conversation he had with his boss about innovative care delivery models, like the value-based care model.

Lisa said, "I keep hearing about this value-based care. Tell me more about it."

"Value-based care is a framework where health systems are paid for the quality and safety of health care provided rather than the number of services provided. There is an emphasis on improving health care outcomes while also reducing costs. Health systems can get incentives for providing better care, lose money for not providing quality and safe care, or get their money for what they were supposed to get. It also impacts the experience of patients and improves the health of the population.

On the other hand, unlike the value-based care model, the fee-for-service model is where health systems are reimbursed for the quantity of services provided.

There are various value-based programs. Some of them focus on reducing readmissions to the hospital, decreasing mortality and improving primary care and chronic care management. Other programs focus on improving patient experience, patient safety, and reducing hospital-acquired conditions."

Lisa, you work as a teacher. Let me use an example related to teaching that can help you better understand the value-based care model. Fee-for-service is like individual tutoring sessions, where payment is made for each session individually. On the other hand, value-based care is like a good educational system that receives payments based on outcomes like student graduation rates, their performance on standardized test scores, attendance rates, teacher development and so on. They are also rated compared to other schools. So, they must focus on the quality of education provided. If their outcomes are not great, student enrollment decreases, and their payments may decrease.

"I liked your analogy, John. I appreciate the way you explained it. I can't believe how illustrations like these can help us understand even complex topics," Lisa remarked. Henry nodded in agreement, already thinking about other thoughtful ways to spread this innovative approach through the community.

Lisa said, "Without realizing it, I walked ten thousand steps at the gym. This was my target for physical activity today. I was so engrossed in our conversation. Maybe we should talk like this more often on crucial topics.

Henry nodded in agreement. Henry and Lisa smiled, inspired by the potential of sharing understanding through vivid metaphors and perspective-building tales.

Chapter 7

How do you know when it's time to stop fighting? John wondered while staring at the ceiling of his hospital room. The question kept repeating in his mind—a puzzle he couldn't quite solve. He had spent months battling his illness, enduring endless treatments and hospital stays, but now he was tired—so very tired. Was it time to stop? To let go? Or was there still something worth holding on to?

The answer wasn't clear, and as he lay there, his thoughts drifted back to his family. They had been by his side through it all, offering support, love, and the strength to keep going. But they couldn't even solve this puzzle for him. This decision, perhaps the most important one he would ever make, had to come from within. John's mind raced through memories, searching for clues, a sign—anything to help him decide. Was there a moment when the fight became too much? When did the benefit outweigh the reward? And if so, had he already passed it?

Continued...

Henry parked his car in the driveway of John's home. The familiar creak of the gate welcomed him as he stepped out of his car. He carried a basket filled with Lisa's homemade flaxseed crackers and mixed fruit jelly, intending to brighten up his Parents' Day with a bit of a taste of home. As he approached the house, he spotted John waving from the patio with a small but warm smile on his face.

"Dad!" Henry called out as he quickened to meet his father at the steps. The two hugged tightly, and the warmth of their love was evident despite the challenges they had been facing. Inside the house, Martha greeted Henry with a hug and a cup of tea.

"These are from Lisa," Henry said as he placed the basket on the kitchen table. "She also printed out some information on the blood thinner you're taking. I thought it might help answer some of your questions." John nodded with a slightly darkened expression.

"I've got some things to show you," John said, lifting his shirt to reveal several bruises scattered across his chest. Look at my hands and legs. There are bruises everywhere. Henry's brow furrowed as he leaned closer to examine the dark patches.

"Dad, these look pretty severe. Are these from the medication?"

John sighed and nodded. "I stopped taking the blood thinner a few days ago. I also noticed blood in my stool and got worried." The smile on his face faded. "Then, I cut myself while fixing a chair, and it just wouldn't stop bleeding. I thought it might be safer to stop."

Martha chimed in; her voice was laced with concern. "I tried to tell him not to stop without talking to the doctor, but you know your dad. He's stubborn as they come."

Henry shook his head, a mixture of worry and frustration evident in his eyes. "Dad, these medications are crucial. Stopping them could lead to something worse. We need to talk to your doctor about this." John sighed again, this time deeper, as if the weight of his health issues were pressing down on him. "I know, son. But it's hard to think straight when you're scared. I'll call the doctor and let them know what's going on."

A few days later, Henry received a call from his father. John's voice was shaky and worried on the other end of the line. "I'm still finding blood in my stool even after stopping the blood thinner, Henry," he confessed, the fear in his voice deep.

"Dad, this isn't something we can ignore," Henry replied, his tone firm but gentle. "You need to see a specialist."

John hesitated, remembering his conversation with his primary care doctor a month ago. The doctor had recommended seeing a gastroenterologist for a screening colonoscopy, but John had dismissed the idea at the time, not wanting to go through another round of tests and appointments. However, the ongoing issues left him with little choice.

"Alright, I'll do it," John finally agreed, the reluctance clear in his voice. Given the urgency of John's symptoms, his primary care doctor managed to secure a quick appointment with a gastroenterologist. The colonoscopy was scheduled within days, and the rapid progression from concern to action left the family little time to prepare.

The day of the procedure arrived, and Martha sat by John's side, holding his hand tightly as they waited. The procedure was over quickly, but the wait for results felt like an eternity. When the gastroenterologist finally returned, his face was grave.

"We found a mass in your colon, John," the doctor said gently. "We've taken biopsy samples, and we'll need to wait for the results to determine the next steps."

The words hung heavily in the room, Martha's grip tightening on John's hand. "What does that mean, doctor?" she asked, her voice barely above a whisper.

"It means we need to be prepared for the possibility of cancer. The mass looked like cancer. Don't come to any conclusions yet. We must wait for the biopsy result to come back," the doctor replied softly.

Martha appeared calm from the outside, but waves of thoughts were crashing into her brain.

The following week brought the confirmation they had dreaded. The biopsy results showed that the mass was indeed cancerous, and further tests revealed that it had spread beyond the colon, seeping into John's abdomen.

John was referred to see an oncologist. The oncologist they met with laid out the treatment options—surgery, chemotherapy, radiation—but there was no denying the grim reality. Due to John's severe heart failure and other medical conditions, the surgical oncologist ruled out surgery, deeming it too risky.

John listened quietly as the oncologist explained the prognosis and the remaining options. "Chemotherapy and radiation are our best chances to slow the cancer. We can't cure the cancer, but we can try to control the further spread of the cancer," the doctor said. "But given your overall health, this will be a difficult journey."

Reluctantly, John agreed to begin chemotherapy, though the prospect filled him with dread. The treatments were grueling, leaving him weaker and more fatigued with each passing day. But the most painful part was the look in Martha's eyes as she watched him suffer; her own strength stretched thin as she stood by his side through every moment.

For the first time in his life, John felt truly defeated, the weight of his illness pressing down on him harder than ever before. The chemotherapy treatments were taking a heavy toll on John's once-strong body. Each chemotherapy session left him exhausted, both physically and emotionally. The constant diarrhea from the treatments weakened him, leaving him dehydrated and fragile. What used to be simple trips to the hospital had now become exhausting ordeals, further draining his already low energy.

John, who had spent most of his life enjoying good health and the freedom it afforded him, found himself trapped in a cycle of medical crises that felt relentless. His already compromised heart required constant adjustments to his medication, which only added to his growing frustration.

Sitting in the hospital room, John couldn't help but reflect on his choices over the years. He had skipped screening tests, ignored his doctors' advice, and neglected his health in ways that now seemed foolish. The weight of regret hung heavily on his shoulders, compounding his physical suffering with a deep emotional burden. Systemic challenges in healthcare also contributed to his current health condition.

The months dragged on, each one more challenging than the last. John's health continued to deteriorate, with hospitalizations becoming an all-too-frequent occurrence. He was having shortness of breath even at rest and with his daily activities.

Dehydration, breathing difficulties, and a host of other ailments kept him in and out of the hospital, draining what little vitality he had left. Frequent blood draws and further tests added more pain. His spirits, once buoyed by hope, were now mired in the reality of his condition.

When his birthday came, it was not celebrated joyfully with friends and family as it had been in the past years, but inside a hospital room. The nurses and hospital staff wished him well and brought a happy birthday balloon, but it wasn't quite the same as celebrating at home.

Even more deeply sad was the fact that he spent his wedding anniversary in that same hospital room, with

Martha by his side, her own strength slowly fading as she watched the man she loved struggle for each breath.

The way of life that John had cherished had been reduced to a small part of what it once was, leaving both him and Martha in a state of silent sadness.

John's decline was not just a series of physical symptoms; it was a transformation of his entire life. What had once been days filled with purpose and activity was now dominated by medical treatments and the sterile environment of hospital rooms. His world had shrunk to the size of a hospital bed, and each visit to the doctor and additional tests seemed to bring more bad news.

During one particularly harrowing hospital stay, John's lungs were filled with a large amount of fluid, making it almost impossible for him to breathe. The doctors had to insert a needle into his lungs to drain the fluid, providing some relief but also highlighting just how fragile his condition had become. The threat of needing a mechanical ventilator loomed large, with no guarantee that he would be able to come off it once his condition stabilized. The prospect of being permanently dependent on machines for survival terrified John.

That night, he lay awake, wrestling with the reality of his situation. His body was failing him in ways he had never imagined, and the constant battle just to breathe left him exhausted, both physically and mentally.

The next morning, the hospitalist visited John's room. The doctor could see the weariness in John's eyes—the toll that this endless cycle of illness had taken. Sitting beside him, the hospitalist gently broached the subject of advance care planning, something that had been mentioned during John's first hospitalization after his cardiac bypass surgery but was quickly set aside at the time.

This time, however, John was ready to listen. The constant visits to the hospital, the treatments that offered little respite, and the knowledge that his condition was only going to worsen had worn him down. The hospitalist spoke with compassion, explaining the concept of "code" status, what it meant, and the realities that came with it.

For the first time, John allowed himself to consider the possibility that it might be time to focus not on extending life at all costs but on the quality of the life he had left. He agreed to speak with the chaplain, hoping to find peace in the decisions ahead.

As John sat quietly in his hospital bed, the hospitalist and chaplain gathered around, prepared to discuss the most difficult decisions he would have to make. They talked about the goals of care and explained the different options available in advance care planning. The words "full code," "modified DNR," and "DNR" hung heavily in the air, each carrying deep implications for John's future.

A "full code," the hospitalist began, "means that we would attempt all lifesaving measures if your heart or breathing were to fail. This includes chest compressions, mechanical ventilation, shocking of the heart, and other aggressive interventions."

John listened carefully, his face unreadable, as the doctor continued. "With a modified DNR, you could choose which interventions you want and do not want when faced with a medical emergency like cardiac arrest or respiratory arrest. You might customize to receive either chest compressions, mechanical ventilation, or other necessary interventions. It's like a middle ground where some measures are taken, but not all."

Finally, the chaplain gently explained the last option. "A DNR, or 'Do Not Resuscitate,' means that we do not attempt resuscitation efforts if your heart or breathing were to stop.

The chaplain also talked about designating a healthcare proxy or medical power of attorney to make decisions if John is unable to make health-related decisions on his own.

John took in all the information, knowing he had to make some important and hard decisions in his life. Martha sat beside him, her hand clasped in his, while Henry stood nearby, his expression somber. This decision was not to be made lightly, and John knew he needed time to reflect on what truly mattered to him.

That evening, the family gathered in the quiet of John's hospital room. The soft beeping of monitors provided a rhythmic backdrop as they discussed the options laid before them. John was resolute in wanting his decisions to reflect his values, his desire for dignity, and his wish to avoid unnecessary suffering.

"I've thought about it," John finally said, his voice steady despite the emotion in his eyes. "I don't want any more aggressive interventions if it comes to that. I want a D.N.R. If my time is up, I want to go peacefully. I don't want rib fractures from chest compressions; I don't want more pain. I don't want further suffering."

Martha squeezed his hand, tears brimming in her eyes, but she nodded in agreement. "We'll do whatever you think is best, John. We just want you to be comfortable."

Henry, though visibly hurt by the decision, also agreed. "We'll support you, Dad, in whatever way you need."

John requested Martha and Henry to be his healthcare proxy or medical power of attorney. They were familiar with John and his preferences. They understood him deeply. If he were ever unable to make health-related decisions, they would act in his best interest, making choices that aligned with what he would have done if he could make decisions for himself.

The next day, John met with the hospitalist again. The decision had been made, and John's wishes were clear. The doctor respected John's choice, appreciating his thoughtful consideration of this difficult topic. The doctor entered the D.N.R. order in John's chart. The nurse placed a D.N.R. band on John's wrist.

During this conversation, the hospitalist gently suggested palliative care, explaining how it could help John navigate the challenges ahead.

"You've been through so much, John," the doctor said softly. "Palliative care can help manage your symptoms and improve your quality of life. It's not just about end-of-life care. It's about supporting you through every stage of your illness. If you agree with palliative care consultation, then I will request them to come and talk with you."

John trusted this doctor, who had been with him through countless hospital visits, always treating him with compassion and understanding.

After a moment's hesitation, John nodded. "Let's do it," he said. "I think it's time. I can have a chat with them."

Later that day, the palliative care doctor visited John. The atmosphere in the room was calm, almost serene, as the doctor sat beside John's bed, taking time to explain the role of palliative care.

"We're here to support you, John," the doctor began. "Our focus is on easing suffering and keeping you comfortable. We work alongside your other doctors, helping to control symptoms like pain, nausea, shortness of breath, and anxiety while also addressing your emotional and spiritual needs. Palliative care also provides support to families, such as assisting families with complex decision-making, understanding treatment options, and aligning care with patients' wishes and values. It can also provide psychological and emotional support."

"Being on palliative care does not mean you have to stop other treatments for your medical condition. You can continue receiving other treatments while still benefiting from palliative care."

John listened, his mind slowly wrapping around this new concept. The idea of receiving care that focused on his comfort rather than just trying to cure him brought a strange sense of relief.

The doctor continued, "Palliative care isn't just for those at the very end of life. It's about enhancing your quality of life at any stage of your illness. We want to help you live as well as possible, for as long as possible."

John nodded, appreciating the doctor's honesty and the clarity of the explanation. The conversation was different from the others he had had with his medical team. This was about more than just medicine; it was about finding peace, even amid struggles.

The distinction between palliative care and hospice was also made clear. While palliative care could be integrated at any stage of his disease, hospice care was reserved for when the prognosis was six months or less if the illness followed its natural course. While you are in hospice care, you can still get treatments for other health conditions, as long as they fit within the hospice care plan and help keep you comfortable.

John felt empowered by the knowledge and understanding that he still had choices and that his care could be tailored to meet his evolving needs.

As the palliative care doctor left, John felt a sense of calm wash over him. For the first time in a long while, he felt in control of his own journey. The path ahead was uncertain, but he knew he wouldn't have to walk alone. Martha and Henry were with him every step of the way, and now, with the support of the palliative care team, he could focus on what mattered most: living each remaining day with dignity and as much comfort as possible.

The palliative care discussion had given John, Martha and Henry a lot to consider. The three of them had always been close, but now their bond felt even stronger as they navigated this incredibly difficult time together.

"I've been thinking a lot," John began, his voice steady but soft. "About everything the doctors have said about what I've been through... I don't want to spend my last days in and out of hospitals hooked up to machines. I want to be at my sweet home and have a quality life with Martha, Scruffy, friends and other family members."

Martha's eyes filled with tears, but she didn't let them fall. Instead, she nodded, her hand resting gently on John's. "Whatever you want, John, we're here for you."

Though clearly struggling with the thought of losing his father, Henry managed a small, supportive smile. "Dad, we just want you to be comfortable and relaxed. If you want to stay home, that's what we'll do."

John looked between the two of them, his heart swelling with gratitude. "*I want to enroll in hospice care,*" he said, the words heavy with significance. "I don't want to keep fighting this battle that I can't win. I want to be in solace."

I want to discuss this with Cara and Michael as well. I want them to give their opinion. I want them to agree with my decision. It's important to me that they also feel at ease and agree with the choices I make.

When the palliative care doctor returned for a follow-up visit the next day, John was ready. Martha and Henry were by his side as he expressed his decision, his voice calm but resolute.

"I've decided to transition to hospice care," John said, meeting the doctor's eyes with quiet determination. I'm tired of the treatments, the hospitals... I just want to be comfortable."

Martha and Henry nodded in agreement, their hands resting on John's shoulders in support. The decision, though heartbreaking, brought a sense of relief to the room. The revolving door of treatments and hospital visits would finally come to an end, and John could focus on what truly mattered — spending his last days in the comfort of his own home, surrounded by the love and care of his family.

But I want my other children to also agree with my decision. The doctor nodded, respecting John's decision and understanding the depth of thought that had gone into it. "We'll make sure that your wishes are honored, John," said the doctor.

The doctor continued, "Having these difficult conversations with family members, especially when they are far away, can be tough. Are you planning to call and speak with them directly, or would you like me to assist with this discussion?"

John requested that a family conference be arranged so the medical staff could address any questions or concerns his family members may have and could find comfort and fully support his decision.

The palliative care doctor understood that family support was crucial for John to agree with his decision to transition to hospice care. The doctor informed the case manager to arrange a family conference so that everyone could voice their perspectives and concerns before making final decisions.

That afternoon, the case manager arranged a family conference. John's loved ones gathered together. Martha and Henry sat by John's side while Cara and Michael joined in via phone. John's nurse, hospitalist, and palliative care physician also participated in the family conference.

The air was thick with the weight of the discussion ahead. These were not easy conversations—talking about end-of-life care never is. But they were necessary, and everyone knew it.

The medical staff and family members introduced themselves. Medical staff thoroughly explained John's medical condition and provided details about his overall prognosis. They also informed the family about John's decision to transition to hospice care.

It was one of the most important conversations John had ever had with all his children. He openly shared his desire to live his final days with dignity and peace, free from the constraints of medical intervention. Martha and Henry listened intently in the room, their hearts heavy with the gravity of the situation but full of love and respect for John's wishes.

"We've seen you suffer so much," Martha said softly, her voice trembling with emotion. "John, all we want is for you to find some relief, to finally feel the weight lift, and to experience the comfort you've needed for so long."

Henry moved, his eyes glistening with unshed tears. "We'll be with you every step of your journey, Dad. Whatever you need, we're here."

Cara and Michael had numerous questions regarding treatment options. They also wanted to learn more about what hospice care entails. The medical staff responded to their questions as thoroughly as possible.

The local family, familiar with John's suffering, agreed with his wish to move forward with hospice care.

However, Cara and Michael, who were less present in John's recent life, were not ready to let go. They advocated for continuing aggressive treatments, believing that every possible measure should be taken to extend John's life.

The conversation was difficult, with each side presenting valid viewpoints rooted in love and concern for John's well-being. The tension in the room was deep as everyone tried to navigate the delicate balance between hope and acceptance.

The complexities of these discussions rarely lend themselves to quick resolutions; they require time, patience, and a willingness to listen deeply. As the conversation progressed, it became clear that more than one meeting might be needed. Each family member had to grapple with their emotions and come to terms with the reality of John's situation.

It was evident that this process would take time and that rushing towards a decision without fully understanding each other's perspectives would only cause more pain. The family left the meeting with much to think about. Martha, Henry, Cara, and Michael all had John's best interests at heart, but they needed to find a way to reconcile their differing views.

The hope was that through open and honest dialogue, with pauses to reflect and revisit the issues, they could come to a resolution that honored John's wishes and strengthened their family bonds.

Over the following days, John wanted Cara and Michael to be involved more in his healthcare decisions, which proved to be a turning point.

Though Cara and Michael had been estranged for years, the gravity of John's condition brought them back into the fold, prompting conversations they hadn't had in a long time. The siblings were united again in their desire to do what was best for John. Cara and Ashley were still unable to set aside their differences and reconnect.

Initially, both Cara and Michael were adamant about pursuing every possible treatment option for their dad, driven by their love for John and a desire to hold onto him for as long as possible.

However, as they continued to discuss the situation, both with family and with the medical team, their perspectives began to shift. They asked more questions, did their own research, and slowly began to understand John's priority: comfort and quality of life over sheer longevity. The realization that what mattered most to John wasn't the length of his life, but the quality of his remaining time was a profound moment for them.

In the end, this open dialogue and willingness to see things from a different perspective led the family to a harmonious resolution. Cara and Michael, once reluctant to let go of active treatment, came to support John's decision to transition to hospice care.

They recognized that the most selfless act of love was to honor John's wishes, even if it meant letting go of their own desires to keep him alive through aggressive treatment. With this new understanding, the family united around John's decision.

A sense of peace settled over them, knowing they were all working together to support John in the way he needed it most. The resolution didn't come easily, but it came with empathy, wisdom, and a deep love for the man who had always been at the heart of their family.

They finally came to the conclusion that hospice was the best decision for John. They all agreed to respect John's wishes. Hospice care will focus on keeping John comfortable, managing his symptoms, and allowing him to live out his days with dignity and peace."

John felt a sense of relief as all his children finally agreed with his decision. He knew the days ahead would be challenging, but he also knew he wouldn't have to face them alone. With Martha, Henry, Cara, and Michael's support, he could now focus on living out his final days on his own terms in the place that had always been his sanctuary.

When the hospitalist returned the next morning, John said with a quiet but firm voice, "I've made my final decision. I want to stay home, surrounded by my family and friends. I want to be comfortable. I'm done with the treatments. I want to be where my heart is. My family also agrees with my decision to transition to hospice care."

The doctor nodded, his expression one of understanding and respect. "We'll make sure that happens, John. We'll work with you and your family to ensure that you receive the care you need on your terms."

With Martha and Henry by his side, John was fully transitioned to hospice care, which marked the beginning of a new chapter."

***

A calm and reassuring hospice nurse came to their home to check on John. She asked how John and Martha were doing and inquired about John's symptoms.

She went on to explain how the hospice routine level of care would work. John listened carefully, Martha by his side, as the nurse outlined to them again what they could expect.

Routine hospice care would allow John to stay in the place he loved, with the added support of a dedicated care team that includes nurses, physicians, case managers, volunteers, nurse aids, and a chaplain; all of them would visit regularly to provide dedicated assistance.

The nurse explained that this set-up would not only provide John with the comfort of being in his own surroundings but would also ease some of the burden on his family, giving them the support they needed to focus on being present with him.

However, the nurse also made sure they understood that if John's condition worsened and required more intensive monitoring, a continuous level of care was an option. This would ensure that John was never without the assistance he needed, even if his condition became more challenging to manage at home. The reassurance that help was always available, even in the middle of the night, gave Martha peace of mind, knowing they wouldn't have to face any difficult moments alone.

The nurse also introduced the concept of respite level of care, a compassionate provision for family caregivers who might need a break from the intense emotional and physical demands of caring for a loved one.

This service would allow Martha and other family members some time to recharge, knowing that John would be well cared for in their brief absence.

Additionally, the nurse mentioned that if symptoms became particularly difficult to manage at home, a general inpatient level of care was available to ensure that John's comfort remained the top priority.

John appreciated the thoroughness of the explanations. The autonomy to reconsider his goals at any time was particularly comforting. The nurse emphasized that the hospice care plan was not set in stone. It could evolve as John's needs and wishes change.

This ongoing evaluation would ensure that John's care was always aligned with his values and desires, giving him control over his journey. John cracked a small joke as the nurse finished her explanation, trying to lighten the heavy atmosphere.

Despite the seriousness of the situation, his hardy spirit shone through, finding a way to bring a little laughter into the room. It was this resilience, this ability to find light even in the darkest times, that had always defined John.

Martha smiled, feeling a bit of the tension ease from her shoulders. She felt reassured knowing that they had the support of a compassionate and skilled hospice team. This journey wasn't one they would have to cross alone; they had partners in their care who would walk with them every step of the way.

As they moved forward, the focus shifted to living fully in each precious moment they had together. The prognosis, though uncertain, became less important than the time they spent together, cherishing each day as it came.

John's decision to transition to hospice care brought a renewed sense of purpose to their time together, filled with empathy, laughter, and the companionship that had always been at the heart of their family's strength.

John spent his days savoring the small moments, sharing a meal with Martha, talking quietly with Henry, chatting with his grandchildren on the phone, listening to music, working in the garage, or simply enjoying the sun's warmth on his face. These were the treasures that filled his heart and gave him the comfort he sought, far beyond any medical intervention.

As John was getting used to his new routine at home, it became clear that this was the right choice for him. The house, once filled with the anxiety of illness, now felt like a sanctuary.

The decision to prioritize John's peace and autonomy brought joy, even in the face of the bittersweet reality Martha knew was coming. There was beauty in this transition, in the way it allowed John to reclaim his life and live it fully, surrounded by those who loved him.

As the days passed, John's health continued to decline, but his spirit remained strong. He found solace in the presence of his family and friends, in the laughter and love that filled the house. Each moment was a gift, a reminder of his life and the love surrounding him.

In the end, it was not the medical interventions or treatments that mattered but the simple, everyday moments shared with loved ones. John's wish to live fully on his own terms was fulfilled. He knew that he was exactly where he wanted to be: at home, surrounded by love, living each day as it came.

With the strength of those bonds carrying him through to the very end.

Chapter 8

John had settled into a routine at home with hospice care, surrounded by the familiarity and comfort of his life. His house in rural Illinois was quiet and peaceful. His faithful dog, Scruffy, stayed by his side, bringing him joy in those precious moments. His friends, who had known John and Martha for decades, continued to check on him, bringing with them the warmth of countless shared memories. They spent time playing card games, talking about random stuff, and simply being present to provide emotional support and love. Their presence through the years, not just in joy but also during sorrow, says a lot about their true friendship.

Martha bustled around the room, arranging cushions and adjusting blankets. "How are you feeling today, love?" she asked, her voice gentle but full of concern.

John managed a tired smile. "I'm okay, Martha. It's nice to stay home with you. Hospice care is really helping me. I'm more comfortable now."

Hospice nurses visited regularly, carefully monitoring John's symptoms and adjusting his medicines to ensure comfort.

A hospice nurse stopped by to assess John's condition and ensure he was comfortable. She was a kind woman with a warm smile.

"Good afternoon, John," the nurse said as she walked in, carrying a small bag of medical supplies. "How's the pain?"

John shrugged. "It's not too bad today. Just a bit achy."

The nurse nodded and started checking his vitals. "I'll make sure your pain is better managed. Let me call the hospice physician and adjust some of your pain medicines. Remember, if you need anything, just let me know."

Martha watched with a grateful look. "Thank you. It really means a lot to us."

The hospice team wasn't only about medical care. They also brought comfort in other ways. Volunteers came by with soothing music and even offered massage therapy. One volunteer played soft tunes on his guitar that made John's face light up with happiness.

"Hey, John," the volunteer said, strumming a gentle melody. "I hope this helps you relax a bit."

John's eyes closed, and he let the music wash over him. "It's beautiful, buddy. Thank you."

Martha looked at the volunteer with appreciation. "It's nice to have this kind of support. It makes everything a little easier."

John had been through a lot in the past year. He had been to hospitals and doctors more times than he could count. After many tough days, he decided it was time to stop all the treatments and just focus on comfort. Now, he was trying to enjoy his time at home with Martha and the care team around him.

One evening, the doorbell rang. It was the case manager and chaplain from the hospice. Martha greeted them warmly.

They smiled and informed Martha they were there to see if they needed any additional support. During their conversation, John mentioned that he sometimes struggled to lie flat in his bed due to shortness of breath. He had to get up and sleep in his recliner.

The case manager immediately offered a solution, promising to arrange a hospital bed that could elevate the head end of the bed, helping to relieve his shortness of breath. Martha's face lit up. "Oh, that's wonderful! Thank you so much." This practical assistance provided reassurance for both John and Martha, easing their concerns about his comfort.

In addition to addressing John's physical needs, the chaplain offered spiritual support by reading scripture. The gentle words provided a sense of peace, not only for John but also for Martha, who found herself relaxing in the quiet moments of reflection. The chaplain's presence was a reminder that hospice care encompassed more than just medical attention—it also attended to the emotional and spiritual well-being of patients and their loved ones.

Martha expressed her appreciation for the holistic care that the hospice provided. She found comfort in knowing that hospice wasn't just focused on John's physical health but also supported her in coping with the emotional aspects of his illness.

The case manager spoke with them about bereavement support that would be available when the time came, which gave Martha a sense of relief, knowing she wouldn't have to face the future alone. Hospice's commitment to caring for both patients and their families deeply resonated with her, reinforcing the value of their compassionate presence during this difficult time.

"If you need any assistance anytime, please call us. We are here to help," said hospice staff.

Martha nodded. "I'll make sure to call if we need anything. Thanks again for checking in."

The case manager and chaplain gave her a reassuring smile. "You're welcome, Martha. Take care, and don't hesitate to reach out if you need us."

With that, they left. Martha felt a bit more at ease knowing they had additional support. She took a deep breath, feeling grateful for the kindness and care extended to them during this time.

John's days were more relaxed now. He could eat what he wanted and cook his favorite meals without worrying about low-salt or low-fat diets. The house was filled with the smell of his favorite dishes. He enjoyed having his family around him, along with friends who came by to visit.

John's friends transformed his home to ensure its safety. They installed bars in the bathroom and hand railings throughout the house so that every corner was secured. They wanted John to move around the house with confidence and not have a fall. They also supported John and Martha in practical and meaningful ways during this time.

***

It was that time of year again—Thanksgiving. Every year, John and Martha eagerly invited their children to their home for a Thanksgiving celebration. However, it had been decades since the family truly celebrated Thanksgiving together. Michael, who had moved to Los Angeles with Ashley, hadn't visited his childhood home since leaving. Cara caught up in her demanding schedule and work commitments and was frequently absent. Despite their hopes, the festive time had turned into a quiet reminder of the distance that had grown between them.

Last year's Thanksgiving was particularly different, marked by stress and worry. John had suffered a cardiac arrest, leaving the family in turmoil as he was admitted to the hospital. His medical scars were a stark reminder of how fragile life had become. Instead of the usual feast and joy, the holiday was overshadowed by concerns for John's health.

This year, though, John was determined to have a joyful Thanksgiving with friends and family. He was excited at the thought of having everyone together again.

John looked at Martha and said with a hopeful smile, "I really want this Thanksgiving to be special. It's been a while since we had the whole family here."

Martha nodded, her eyes shining. "I know, John. I've been making calls to everyone. Michael and Ashley are coming with their girls. It'll be the first time we meet them in person."

John's face lit up. "That's wonderful! I've been looking forward to meeting our granddaughters. And Cara and her family will be here too. It's going to be great."

John's excitement was clear. He was especially thrilled about making his famous pumpkin pie. "I'm going to bake the best pumpkin pie ever. I want everyone to enjoy it just like Sam enjoys and appreciates it."

Martha smiled. "I know you will. You always make the most delicious pumpkin pie."

Martha worked hard to prepare for the big day. John helped as much as he could. The house was decorated with autumn leaves and pumpkins, creating a warm and festive atmosphere. Martha made sure there was plenty of food, and John looked forward to baking his pie.

As Thanksgiving drew nearer, John's health was stable. He was in good spirits, and the thought of having the family gathered around made him feel content. The hospice team continued to visit, ensuring he was comfortable and symptom-free.

John and Martha were thrilled that everyone had agreed to come for Thanksgiving this year. They hoped that the gathering would be more than just a celebration of the holiday. They were especially hopeful that Cara and Ashley might put aside their differences and start mending their strained relationship.

Despite the challenges of the past year, Cara and Michael were talking more because of John's medical condition. Cara and Ashley still hadn't found a way to get along. John and Martha wished for a family reunion where everyone could come together, heal old wounds, and enjoy each other's company. They wanted this Thanksgiving to be a chance for everyone to reconnect.

John sat in the living room, and Scruffy curled up beside him. The old dog had been a constant companion since John came home. Scruffy followed John everywhere, sensing that something was amiss.

The bond between them was deep. John would often pat Scruffy's head and whisper, "You're my best friend, you know that?" Scruffy would wag his tail and nuzzle close to him as if understanding every word.

Henry went to the airport to pick up Michael's family. Henry hadn't seen Michael's children in person, so when he finally saw them, his heart swelled with joy.

Michael and Henry hugged; their connection instantly rekindled. Tears rolled in Michael's eyes as a flood of childhood memories played in front of him. Though life had taken him far from his childhood place, his heart had never truly left. His rural childhood home was always special for him.

Henry gave a high-five to the kids. "Hello, Emily and Sofia. Do you know who I am?" asked Henry.

"Yes, you are our Uncle Henry," the kids replied.

"Sam and Lisa will be thrilled to see you," Henry said.

Michael's wife, Ashley, was also delighted to meet Henry. "Henry, it's been ages! You look exactly the same as I remember," she laughed, giving him a warm hug. She also expressed her eagerness to meet Lisa and Sam. "I can't wait to talk to them," she said, regretfully adding, "I'm sorry I didn't make more of an effort to stay connected."

Henry, always understanding, gently reassured her, "No worries, Ashley. In the end, we're all family. Troubles and conflicts happen, but what's important is that we find our way back to each other."

Henry, trying to lighten the mood, asked the kids if they liked candy. They responded with a resounding "Yes!" and bright smiles. Later, as they were heading to the car, Henry handed the kids chocolates, adding a sweet touch to the reunion, and their laughter filled the space.

As they drove from the airport to John and Martha's house, the car was filled with chatter.

"Do you remember we used to play here as kids?" Ashley asked, looking out the window.

Henry nodded. "I sure do. It feels like those days were just yesterday."

Martha and John were happy to see Michael and his family. With a wide smile, John gave Michael's kids, Emily and Sofia, a warm hug, and the kids enthusiastically hugged him, calling him "Grandpa." The warmth of their embrace brought tears to his eyes.

Cara, too, took a break from her busy schedule for the week of Thanksgiving. Her family arrived at the childhood home. "It's nice to be back home," she said.

The house was now bustling with John, Martha, their children, and grandchildren. The atmosphere was lively, with lots of laughter, storytelling, and cooking together.

"Everyone's here!" Martha exclaimed happily. "It's so wonderful to have the house full again."

The children quickly bonded, running around in the backyard and playing on the tractor. Sam, who had never met Michael's daughters before, was excitedly showing them around. "This is my favorite spot!" she said, pointing to the swing set.

Daniel, Cara's son, joined in. "Let's see who can swing the highest!" he challenged.

As the evening approached, Martha brought out a photo album. "I thought you might like to see some old pictures of your parents when they were your age," she said, opening the photo album.

Despite the joyful gathering, a quiet tension remained between Cara and Ashley. They exchanged glances but did not speak. Henry sensed that both Cara and Ashley wanted to reconnect, but their egos kept them apart. He knew that once they began talking, their old friendship would rekindle. After all, Cara and Ashley had been best friends growing up, sharing many memories and dreams.

The kids gathered around eagerly. "Look at this one!" Martha said, pointing to a photo of a young Cara and Ashley playing together. "They were best friends and always up for some adventure," John observed the old photos with a smile. He saw how Cara and Ashley were often together, laughing and playing. He hoped that seeing these old memories might help bridge the gap between them now.

Martha pointed out another photo. "And here's one of Daniel's mom and Michael. They were always so full of energy." Daniel looked at the photo and said with a smile, "I can't believe Mom was ever that small!" Everyone laughed, and for a moment, the room was filled with a sense of nostalgia and joy. John and Martha watched with contented hearts, glad to see their family coming together and sharing these precious memories.

The next morning, the house was bustling with excitement. After a hearty breakfast, the kids, eager for adventure, approached Henry with wide eyes. "We want to see the town," Michael's daughters said, bouncing on their toes. "And we want to visit the school where our parents went!"

Daniel nodded eagerly. "I want to see it all, too. Mom, can you come with us?"

Cara looked up from her coffee and smiled. "Okay, I'll come too," she agreed with a nod.

Ashley's kids also wanted their mom to join them. She also agreed. So, Henry, with his big SUV, made room for everyone. Sam decided to join them as well. "All right then, let's head out. I'll show you around," said Henry.

The SUV bumped along the rural roads. Henry began pointing out various landmarks. "Emily and Sofia, here's the old bridge where your mom and dad used to play. And over there is the path they took to come to school every day." The kids leaned forward, eyes wide with curiosity.

"Is that where Mom and Dad went to school?" Michael's daughter asked, looking out the window.

"Yes, that's the very same school," Henry replied. "It's not very big, but it has a lot of history."

They arrived at the school; a quaint building surrounded by open fields. Henry parked the car and led them inside. The children marveled at the small classrooms and old-fashioned desks. "Wow, this is so different from our schools," Michael's daughter said, looking around in awe. Cara watched her son explore with a mix of nostalgia and hope, remembering her own school days and wishing for a smoother relationship with Ashley.

Henry showed the kids a display on the wall. "Look at these old photos. Here's a picture of your parents when they were your age." The kids gathered around, pointing and laughing at the pictures of their parents as children. "This is so cool!" Daniel exclaimed, studying the images closely.

Ashley and Cara stood quietly, each lost in their own thoughts as they glanced around the familiar spaces—the theater, the classroom, the gym, and the playground. Memories of their shared laughter and innocent days flooded back, stirring a deep sense of nostalgia.

"Where did our innocent days go?" Ashley wondered, thinking of the bond they once had as best friends.

Cara, too, was caught in the warmth of those memories, remembering the closeness they had shared. She knew that her pride had built the walls between her and Ashley, preventing her from reaching out. Despite their mutual longing to reconnect, neither of them could take that first step. So, they stood, each waiting for the other to make the move that could bring them back together.

As the tour continued, Henry drove them up the mountains and across the river, giving them a taste of the rural life their parents had once known. The kids took in the sights with excitement, enjoying the adventure of discovering their parents' past.

When they returned to the house, John and Martha greeted them with smiles. "How was the tour?" John asked, looking at the beaming faces of the children.

"It was amazing!" the kids said, jumping up and down. "We saw everything!"

The day's adventures left everyone feeling warm and reflective. Going through all the nostalgia, Cara and Ashley couldn't hold it in any longer. They finally decided to share a quiet moment together in the living room, surrounded by the warmth of family.

"Cara," Ashley began, breaking the silence, "I've been thinking a lot today. It's hard to believe how much time has passed and how we've let our differences get in the way." Cara looked at Ashley with a mix of sadness and understanding. "I feel the same way. I've been stubborn and held onto my pride. I'm sorry for that."

Ashley reached out, taking Cara's hand. "I'm sorry, too. I missed our friendship and all those memories we shared." Tears rolled down both women's cheeks as they embraced. Their long-standing rift was starting to heal.

John and Martha watched from a distance. Their hearts full of relief and joy. The family, reunited and mending old wounds, gathered around the dinner table. Their shared history brought them closer together.

Ashley also apologized for not taking the initiative to reach out sooner and for not trying to mend their relationship over the years. Cara, in turn, expressed regret for her past harshness toward Ashley and Michael. She admitted she had been rude, questioning Michael's potential and criticizing their relationship. Now, Cara understood the depth of the love that Ashley and Michael had shared since their teenage years. She was genuinely proud of them for maintaining their strong bond despite the struggles they faced. She admired how they had persevered through hardships and found happiness, raising two beautiful children.

With tears wiped away, Cara and Ashley began talking openly. The atmosphere in the house felt lighter, and the two women felt a renewed sense of connection. The missing piece in their family puzzle seemed to have been found, completing the picture of their togetherness.

John reflected on the day as one of the best of his life, surrounded by his loved ones and feeling a deep sense of happiness. For a moment, he forgot about the medical challenges he had endured. The joy of having his family reunited and at peace brought him immense comfort.

John sat at the head of the table, a broad smile stretching across his face. The warmth of Thanksgiving was all around him. "This is the best day ever," he said, his eyes shining with happiness.

Martha moved around the kitchen, finishing up the last touches on the Thanksgiving feast. "John, you always say that" she replied with a laugh, "but I think this year you might be right."

The family and their friends gathered around the dining table. A beautiful spread of turkey, stuffing, and all the fixings laid out before them. Lisa, who was known for her culinary skills, had teamed up with Martha to prepare the meal.

"You did a great job on that pie, Dad," Lisa said as she admired the pumpkin pie. John beamed. "Thanks, Lisa. It's one of my favorites."

As they enjoyed their meal, the conversation flowed freely. Everyone shared stories and memories. Laughter rang through the room. The children, full of excitement from their earlier tour of the town and school, chattered about their favorite parts of the day.

After dinner, Martha brought out a box from a shelf in the corner of the room. "I have something special to share," she said, a nostalgic gleam in her eye. "Do you all remember the songs Henry, Cara, and Michael wrote when they were kids?"

The room fell silent as the old songs were brought out. The papers, yellowed with age, were covered in the handwritten lyrics of the childhood band that never quite got off the ground.

Henry's eyes lit up as he looked at the papers. "I can't believe you kept these, Mom."

Cara picked up a sheet and laughed softly. "We were so ambitious. I remember practicing these in the garage." Michael nodded, grinning. "Let's do it. Let's play these songs like we always wanted to."

They quickly set up their old instruments—Henry on drums, Michael on guitar, and Cara on piano and vocals. The children and guests gathered around, curious and excited.

John and Martha watched with pride as the trio started to perform. "Ready?" Henry asked, looking at Cara and Michael.

"Ready!" Cara and Michael answered in unison.

As the first notes filled the room, a wave of nostalgia swept over the family. The songs, though simple and a bit rusty, were filled with the joy and dreams of their younger selves. The children watched in awe, their faces lighting up with the infectious energy of their parents' performance. "This is so cool!" Daniel exclaimed; his eyes wide as he watched his mom play.

The performance was a hit. The guests clapped along, and the children were having fun, soaking up the special moment. When they finished, the room erupted in applause and cheers.

"That was amazing!" Lisa shouted, joining in the applause.

John wiped a tear from his eye. "This has been one of the best Thanksgivings ever," he said, his voice thick with emotion. "Having everyone together, reliving these memories. It means the world to me."

Martha hugged John tightly. "I agree. It's moments like these that make everything worthwhile."

As the evening wore on, the house was alive with laughter and music. Everyone danced with abandon. John, in particular, moved with an enthusiasm that seemed to defy the limitations of his recent health struggles. "Dance like there's no tomorrow!" he called out, twirling around with a wide grin.

Ashley and the kids joined in, their laughter mingling with the lively music. Ashley, being a good dancer, showed her cool dance moves. She also made Lisa and Martha dance to the music. Scruffy also showed his moves.

Martha watched with delight, her heart swelling with happiness as she saw everyone enjoying themselves. The whole house was filled with energy and celebration.

The family and friends sat together, basking in the warmth and joy of their shared history. The music, laughter, and love filled the house, making it a Thanksgiving to remember.

Later that night, after the friends had left and the children had been tucked into bed, the house quieted down. John and Henry found themselves alone in the living room. They were surrounded by the soft glow of the lamplight. They sat together, reflecting on the day's events.

"I can't remember the last time I felt this happy," John said, his voice filled with contentment. "It's been a long time coming, but having everyone together like this, it's been incredible."

Henry nodded, and a warm smile was on his face. "It really has been. It's wonderful to see the family coming together like this, especially after everything we've been through."

John looked at Henry with a thoughtful expression. "Henry, I want to share something special with you. It's my secret pumpkin pie recipe. I want you to have it, just in case I'm not around for the next Thanksgiving. I want Sam to enjoy it, too."

Henry's eyes grew misty. "Dad, you're going to be around for a long time. I know you will be." John shook his head gently. "It's important to me that Sam gets to experience this recipe. It's been a tradition for us, and I want it to continue."

Henry took a deep breath, his emotions swelling. "I'll make sure Sam gets it. Thank you, Dad."

John handed Henry a carefully folded piece of paper with the recipe written on it. "It's my little secret," he said with a smile. "Now, you better make it just like I do."

Henry took the paper, his heart full. "I promise. Goodnight, Dad." "Goodnight, Henry," John said, patting his son's shoulder. "And thank you for everything. It's been a perfect day."

They shared a warm hug before Henry headed to bed. As he climbed into his own bed, the day's events replayed in John's mind, filling him with a deep sense of satisfaction.

In the quiet hours of the night, Martha woke up and found herself unable to sleep. She thought about the day's events and the happiness that had filled their home. She quietly got up, deciding to check on everyone and savor the peaceful moment. Seeing the house so full of love and joy, she felt a deep sense of gratitude. As she stood in the doorway, looking at her family, she knew this Thanksgiving would be a cherished memory for years to come. It had been a day of healing, celebration, and reconnection—a true reminder of the importance of family.

Martha quietly returned to her room. She leaned down gently, placing a tender kiss on John's forehead. "Good night, my love," she whispered softly, her voice full of affection. "Have a good sleep." With a lingering gaze, she tucked the blanket around him, as she watched him drift off into a peaceful sleep.

The next morning, Martha woke up early and checked on John. When she found him still in bed, worry set in. Gently shaking him, she realized something was terribly wrong.

"John, wake up," she said, her voice trembling. When John didn't stir, Martha's heart sank. She hurried to wake Henry and the others. "Henry, come quickly," she called out. Henry, along with Cara, Michael, Scruffy, and the rest of the family, rushed to John's side. They found him lying peacefully, but there was no pulse.

Cara's face grew pale as she checked John's pulse and confirmed the worst. "There's no pulse," she whispered, tears streaming down her cheeks. Henry stood silent; his eyes filled with grief. He knew John had passed away in his sleep.

Scruffy sat beside John's bed with tears in his eyes.

Though their hearts were heavy with sorrow, there was a sense of quiet comfort knowing that John had left this world surrounded by his loved ones, just as he had wished. His final days had been filled with joy, celebration, and the warmth of friends and family.

The funeral was an emotional tribute to John's life. Martha had arranged for his favorite music to be played. Country songs that had been a part of his life for as long as anyone could remember. The strains of a familiar old tune filled the air, a gentle reminder of the man they had loved. As part of the service, there was a special tribute to John's unique bond with his granddaughter Sam. Sam introduced John to Taylor Swift's music, and John came to enjoy her songs.

At John's funeral, the family and friends gathered to honor his memory and reflect on the life he had lived.

Cara, moved by the loss and driven by her love for her family, made a generous decision to cover all of John's medical bills.

Henry's family, in turn, stepped up to ensure Martha would be well cared for. Lisa, who had always treated Martha like a second mother, assured her that they would look after her with the same love and attention.

Michael promised to maintain family bonds moving forward, knowing that once our loved ones are gone, we can't bring them back.

The family made a heartfelt agreement to continue their tradition of gathering every year for Thanksgiving at John's place. This annual gathering would serve as a tribute to him and a way to keep the family connected.

Henry took a moment to reflect on the lessons he had learned throughout this journey. Standing before his family, he spoke with a mix of humility and insight. "I've learned so much through this experience," Henry began, his voice steady despite the weight of his words. "The healthcare staff did an incredible work, even when faced with daunting challenges. One of the biggest lessons is the importance of good communication in healthcare."

He continued, "I've come to understand the vital role of quality and safety in healthcare and how essential it is to keep up with primary care visits. Mental health is just as important as physical health. Medication compliance, regular exercise, and a balanced diet are also vital. A holistic approach to managing health is crucial."

As we navigate the challenges of health care, it's clear that innovation and policy changes are essential to overcoming the obstacles that lie ahead. Healthcare itself is challenging and complex, often difficult to fully grasp. Improving health literacy is so vital. Helping people understand the intricacies of health care in simple, relatable terms can make the difference in providing proper care and support.

Henry's eyes softened as he spoke about the importance of advanced care planning and the value of palliative and hospice care. "It's not just about the quantity of life, but the quality of life."

"These are the things I've learned firsthand, and they've made me appreciate the dedication of everyone involved in our healthcare system.

I have also come to realize how deeply family, friends, and community can come together in times of need. The bonds we share with our families, friends, and communities have a profound impact on our overall well-being. The relationships we nurture, especially with our loved ones, can significantly influence our health.

Our parents cared for us when we were vulnerable, and it's our responsibility to care for them when they need us, particularly when it comes to their health.

Amid all these complexities, love remains an essential and beautiful dimension of life. It comes in many forms and deserves to be cherished. Do not let our differences interfere with our human relationships. There is a unique beauty in unity, in coming together despite challenges, and appreciating the bonds that tie us to one another."

The family listened in solemn agreement, reflecting on their own experiences and the impact of John's passing. With a sense of resolve, they embraced the promise of staying connected and maintaining their tradition.

Martha looked around at the faces of her family and friends, reflecting on the deep impact John had made on all of them. The pain of his loss was deep, but the love and memories they shared provided solace. In the quiet moments of the funeral, Martha found a sense of peace, knowing that John's final days had been filled with the love and joy he had always cherished.

The day ended with a feeling of bittersweet farewell. As the family said their goodbyes, they were comforted by the knowledge that John had lived his life fully, surrounded by those he loved most. The music played on, a tribute to a life well-lived and a man who would be deeply missed.

After saying goodbye, everyone felt that, while John would be greatly missed, his impact would remain through the lessons he taught and the closeness of friends and family. The strong bonds and memories made during this time showed how important his life was.

As the family went back to their routines, they not only felt the sadness of his loss but also a deeper appreciation for family and the value of spending time together. John's legacy of love and strength would guide them, reminding them of the power of their connections and the happiness in their shared moments.

Milton Keynes UK
Ingram Content Group UK Ltd.
UKHW022243201124
451476UK00019B/236

9 798330 547326